VISITATION EVANGELISM

Visitation Evangelism

ITS METHODS AND RESULTS

By
A. EARL KERNAHAN, D.D.

Foreword by
BISHOP EDWIN H. HUGHES, D.D. LL. D.;
Methodist Episcopal Church

New York   Chicago
Fleming H. Revell Company
London and Edinburgh

Printed in the United States of America

New York: 158 Fifth Avenue
Chicago: 17 North Wabash Ave.
London: 21 Paternoster Square
Edinburgh: 75 Princes Street

To My Wife, Susanna Elizabeth Kernahan,
Who Has Inspired and Blessed Every Day of
My Ministry Since the First Day That We
Met, This Book Is Affectionately Dedicated.

GOD'S COMMISSIONER

(DEDICATED TO REV. A. E. KERNAHAN, D.D.)

From out the west, young oracle of God,
  He early came to range among the schools,
  With purpose deep,—not that of prating fools,—
To temper heart, and win divining-rod;
To grasp the shepherd's staff; to make a clod
  Grow verdant from the truth; and to the pools
  Of crystal life to lead the sheep he rules
With gentle words,—the growing flock of God.
Soon spoke the voice of Him who masters men:—
  " You have I chosen for a greater task,—
    Apostles to depute in your own right,
To wake the glow of Pentecost again,
  Cold hearts to fire, for high desire to ask,
    And bear twin torches through the shadowy
      night."

CLARENCE M. GALLUP, D.D.,
Pastor of Central Baptist Church.

63 Arlington Avenue,
Providence, R. I.

Foreword

IT is a sign of the hunger on the part of ministers and laymen for evangelistic knowledge and evangelistic inspiration, that books on the general subject have a ready welcome and a wide circulation. One could give the titles of many volumes that have appeared in the recent years dealing with the technique of this holy matter, while the volumes of men like Harold Begbie and others, recording the romances of evangelism in the re-making of actual souls, have found their way to laboratory libraries and to polite parlour tables.

Some books on the subject, it must be confessed, were too academic to be much worth while. Indeed no book, whether it be the recital of the stories of evangelism or a discussion of its methods, can be effective if it be a cloistered production. Any persuasive and revealing treatise must always come out of actual life. Evangelists are not abstract. On the contrary, they are most vital. Edwards, Finney, Wesley, Moody,—these men were not shadowy figures, peeping out from an imagined world. They were rather rigourous "humans."

Indeed, Drummond said that Moody was the greatest " human " that Drummond himself ever knew!

And books on evangelism must be like these personal figures of evangelism; they, too, must be fashioned in life. The writer recalls no work on the subject that has had wide and effective currency, unless it came out of real travail with real souls by real messengers. The theorist is not at home in this field. Amateurishness is most amateurish here; and the academician is most academic. Somehow, the man must go into the book, and the reader must be able to say, " He, himself, did the work."

Here is another book on Evangelism; presenting a method so old and apostolic as to be new. It applies the way of the financial canvass to the higher commerce of the Kingdom. Surely the book will be like Christ in one respect if it send out the modern disciples, as He sent the ancient, " two by two," so that these disciples may return as apostles, with glowing faces and wondrous tales of spiritual conquest.

Dr. Kernahan has not attempted any learned treatise. But he has given an evangelistic narrative, and out of the narrative the wise reader will extract the method himself. I have long been certain that, if we are to be truly apostolic, we must return to the visitation plan. It does not contradict the method of mass evangelism. That method faded because it was too long the sole dependence of some churches, and, also, because it met the competitions of growingly complex life. Yet Pentecost and Antioch are in the New Testament, and they will the more surely return to the modern Church, if this visitation plan be used with faithfulness.

Therefore, I delight to put my name and word in the front of this book; and to have a wee part in sending it on to those eager searchers for the finer fashions and the higher moods of the evangelistic Life.

EDWIN H. HUGHES.

Episcopal Residence,
Chicago, Ill.

Introduction

AFTER a most useful service as Chaplain of the First Division, A. E. F., Mr. Kernahan came to Boston, where he was Pastor of one of the leading churches of his denomination. By his force, his learning, his attractive personality and his evident devout purpose he naturally took a position of real leadership in the whole community. We are better because he lived and worked among us. My testimony may be prejudiced because I have come to regard him as a friend, but you will gain the same opinion from all those who know of his work in Boston or Northampton, Mass., where he lived before entering the army. In my judgment he is an eloquent and convincing advocate of the fundamentals which we most need in America today.

CHANNING H. COX,
Governor of the Commonwealth
of Massachusetts.

Contents

I

THE NEW METHOD

II

HOW TO ORGANIZE

III

THE DISCOVERIES OF VISITATION EVANGELISM

IV

GOD'S GREATEST HUMAN RESOURCE

V

THE EVANGELISM OF THE CHANGELESS CHRIST

I

THE NEW METHOD

I

THE EVOLUTION OF THE METHOD

THE one sure proof of a man's call to the ministry is his ability to win people to Christ. This has been my supreme conviction since the first thought of the ministry entered my mind; consequently, the constant passion of my life has been to succeed here.

The background of my religious experience was set in the Middle West. The people of this section are particularly evangelistic. I commenced preaching before I was sixteen years of age, and very naturally threw myself with enthusiasm into the only method of evangelism that the people of this region knew anything about—namely, mass evangelism. It was my custom to hold one series of meetings in my own church and another in the church of some neighbouring pastor every year. There seemed to be no other way to attempt to win that portion of our church responsibility which we did not win by the regular church program of worship and teaching. God gave us considerable success. The Methodist Episcopal Church accepted this type of work without any question.

In 1913, I went to New England. I carried with

15

me some carefully-thought-out conclusions about
the mass method of evangelism. One was that we
were spending altogether too much time at head-
quarters. For instance: the last work that I was
engaged in before leaving for New England was a
series of four weeks of meetings. We kept as
careful a record as possible of those who attended
these meetings. I preached every evening, includ-
ing Saturday, and three times on Sunday, each
week. We found that ninety-six per cent. of the
people who attended these meetings were already
members of the church. You see, I had prepared a
series of sermons for the purpose of winning those
whom we did not win by regular church work to
Christian discipleship. I had preached them to a
crowd ninety-six per cent. of whom were already
Christians. That was a waste of time. Another
conclusion was, that those who attended the services
were not using the spirituality that was generated
in those services, for the purpose intended. It is
very clear that this new urge and zeal should be
used to persuade men and women to become Christians. As a matter of fact, most of the people who
were inspired by these meetings, hugged that spiritual experience up to themselves and dismissed
their whole thought of responsibility for others by
saying, " Wasn't it a blessed meeting!" If they
had taken this new power and applied it to the task
of persuading others to become Christians, then the
meeting would have been much more successful.

I found New England altogether different from the Middle West. It was different in its attitude toward religion in general. The people were less emotional. They did not seem to have much respect for emotion itself. If the emotion accompanied some big decision, well and good. If it was emotion for emotion's sake alone—then it was taboo.

The Methodists of New England questioned seriously whether the mass method of evangelism was the only legitimate one. They had not thought out any other method, but they had become prejudiced against this one. Many of the churches had suffered painful disillusionments in their experiences with professional evangelists. I found, therefore, that it was necessary, if I were to have a series of meetings, first, to convert the members of my church to this method, and then to convert the people in the community. To do this at all successfully, I must spend a very large amount of money in a publicity program. I justified the expenditure of this money by saying, " Who can measure the worth of a soul ? "

I continued to hold these meetings in New England, not because I was satisfied with them, but because it was the only method with which people were acquainted. Now and then, I heard men speak of personal evangelism, but they meant one of two things: either that a few persons spoke to their friends in some meeting, or that the pastor spoke to individuals in the course of his parish work.

After three years in New England I went to New York City for a year. This was just preceding the visit of Billy Sunday to New York. I had the pleasure of assisting in setting up the district prayer-meetings which are always held preparatory to his work. We looked forward to his coming with high anticipation. I must confess that I was determined to make a close study of his method, so as to find out just what effect a campaign of this kind had upon the local churches. I found that the campaign was of tremendous inspirational value to the city in general, that it had a tendency to make people more militant in their Christian convictions; but, these assertions are true only when they are regarded from an inspirational point of view.

The effect of the campaign upon the churches was discouraging in many respects. The cards that were sent to the various pastors, in a large percentage of cases, carried the names of people who were already church members. Many of the cards which were not of this class were discouraging to the highest degree. People had become wrought upon emotionally. Certain psychological advantages had been taken. They had been won to the spell of a meeting instead of being won to a clear, intelligent acceptance of Jesus as their Saviour. A very small percentage of those reported as won actually joined the churches, and even many of these were very hard to care for. They had been persuaded to make their decision in a very abnormal situation. They were saying before long: "Our pastor is not like Billy Sunday."

Probably no experience could have helped me more to come to the conclusion that was already forming in my mind, namely, that sensational evangelism has tremendous hazards, handicaps, and regrettable experiences.

After a year in New York I went back near Boston, Mass. Billy Sunday held a campaign there also. I studied his work again and found exactly the same situation. The largest number of the cards carried the names of people who were already members of the Church; very few new men joined the Church; many of those who did, were very hard to train and establish in it.

War was declared and I became a chaplain in the Army. I found that my work here had to be done almost entirely by personal contact. I noticed that the boys who were won to Christ by the personal contact method were much firmer in their decisions. They had a tendency to remain faithful to their vows. The boys who raised their hands or came forward in big mass meetings were, to an alarming extent, temporary in their loyalties and unfaithful in their vows. I had the rare privilege of talking to literally thousands of men individually. They threw away their prejudices about religion and were open to a frank presentation when we talked to them personally. They were often indifferent and irresponsive when we talked to them in a group, but they told us their problems, literally laid bare to us the most intimate secrets of their lives, when we sat by their sides or walked with them. Here we could deal with their one problem, or their several problems, in a definite, positive way—which obtained results.

I came back to America with the conviction that if we could get any considerable number of men in our Church to enlist in this work, we would usher in a new epoch in the history of the Christian body.

I had been assigned to the pulpit of a church in Boston before I started home from Germany. I found myself situated in a beautiful, prosperous, residential section of the city. The people were comfortable, contented, and conservative. In other words, I had been appointed to work in a community which was quite likely to confirm my conclusions that mass evangelism did not reach many types of people.

It was my pleasure a few months after assuming the duties of this pastorate, to preach for two weeks in Trinity Methodist Episcopal Church, of Norwich, Conn. The Rev. W. H. Bath, District Superintendent of the Norwich District, New England Southern Conference, of the Methodist Episcopal Church, requested me to attempt to "revive" the people. "Just convince them that evangelism is still a live issue," he said. "Don't try to hold the old-fashioned meetings. They will not respond. Make them know, make them feel that Jesus can save today as He has always saved men—but do not prejudice them by insisting on the old method."

I went to Trinity Church with the desire to win men by a type of educational evangelism. I arrived on a Monday night, and although there were six other churches combined with Trinity Church, we had the large number of seventeen at our first meeting! I was absolutely determined to get a crowd—and I did. The sexton thanked me for getting the seats in the gallery dusted off once more. Many of the members said on the first Sunday we had the largest crowds that had attended service since Bishop Quayle presided there, nine years before.

The questions that arose in my mind, however, were these: "Are we spending too much time just to get a crowd? Would it not be better to go to the homes and uncover the religious aspirations and hungers of the individual; question them about their local Christian responsibility; get them to decide to accept Jesus Christ and His program for them in that community, and in the world; and then invite them to church? They should then have something to go for."

When we came to the conclusion of these meetings, I sat down and analysed the results carefully.

I had been the preacher—I could violently criticise, and nobody could object. I came to several conclusions. The first one was that we had made no real impression on the life of that portion of our constituency for which the meeting was held; that we had won no whole families to the Christian program of living. Just now and then one out of a family had been won. Another conclusion was that if you were to visit Trinity Church six months from that date, it would be difficult to discover any difference in the spiritual life of the people in the church. Another conclusion was that the old members of the church were not prepared to assimilate these newcomers into the body and spirit of the Christian Kingdom.

I went back to my own pulpit in Boston, held a series of meetings for my own people. At the conclusion of this special endeavour, I said: "I will never hold another series of evangelistic services for the specific purpose of winning people to a public decision for Christ. I will, now and then, hold a series of meetings for inspirational, educational, and cultural purposes; but not for the purpose of converting men to Christian discipleship." I had always been practical in my ministry. I did not believe in discarding one method without having some other method to substitute for it. The situation was becoming serious. I was absolutely determined to find some way to accomplish this work satisfactorily. It occurred to me that it would be wise to try and discover just how Jesus did this work. I found clearly, to my delight, that Jesus won every outstanding follower by the personal contact method. (A full exposition of this fact in the fourth chapter of this book.) I also found that the immediate followers of Jesus carried on their work in evangelism by personal interviews. There is the record that St. Peter preached and thousands were won; but if you will read that record carefully, you will find that the other followers, while he was preaching, were running here and there and everywhere, inviting men and women to become followers of Jesus. You will remember Jesus sent the Seventy, two by two, to carry on this work. They came back so hilariously happy that they said: "Even the evil spirits are subject unto us."

After I had found that Jesus did the work thus, and that His immediate disciples did the work thus, I turned my attention to the early history of the Church and I found that here, again, there was unmistakable evidence that during the phenomenal growth of the Church in those early years, the work was done by religious conversations in which one Christian talked to another, or, at the most, to a few. The laws of the day made it impossible to hold mass meetings, and yet, during this very period, one of the striking miracles in the history of the Christian church occurred; namely, the conversion of the Roman Empire.

I was now convinced that it was time to experiment. I could tell the laymen that Jesus won His followers by personal interview, that His immediate disciples found romance and achieved success in this kind of work, that the members of the Early Church extended the borders of the church and accordingly converted the Roman Empire through quiet, persistent, passionate, religious conversation. I would ask them: " Is there any reason why the early followers of Jesus could do this, and not we? Did they have any authority that we do not have? Could they anticipate success any more than we can? " I was quite sure that Jesus' disciples of today could do anything that the early disciples did. I was of the opinion that we had just as much authority as Peter, or John, or Matthew, or Nathanael. I was persuaded that we had a far greater promise of success than they had. We had not been preaching and teaching for nineteen hundred years without building up a certain religious background. We could appeal to society on these grounds with every reason to believe that we would get a response that the early disciples could not have expected to get.

Just at this time I met a man by the name of Guy H. Black. He had been experimenting in exactly the same field. We had come to exactly the same conclusions. We worked together in the city of Chicago for several weeks. Our results were a revelation to the Christians there.

I resigned from my pastorate and consecrated my life to the purpose of demonstrating what laymen can do towards winning the fifty million or more people in our country who are now outside of the Roman Catholic, Jewish, and Protestant Churches to friendship with Jesus Christ and membership in some body of His followers.

II

SOME UNDERLYING ASSUMPTIONS

IT is safe to assume that Jesus' Name is not strange. It is very difficult to find a man anywhere who does not know perfectly well what you mean when you ask him to become a Christian. I am not talking about a perfect understanding of all the individual and social responsibilities that one has as a follower of Christ—I am speaking about the first step in the Christian life. We assume, therefore, in this work, that men and women, everywhere, have been in such relationship to Christian preaching and teaching that they understand the invitation when it is given to them. We assume also that members of every denomination under the shining sun are talking about some type of Christian experience which is absolutely valid; that we do not, therefore, expect all to have the same experience; that it is our duty and privilege to get them to look upon Christ and have their own experience. We must consequently respect the other person's religious background.

In South Manchester, Conn., one of the first teams of two to go out to do this work was made up of an English woman and a German woman.

The first call they made was in a German home. The people in this family had had their religious experience and training in the German Lutheran Church, but had ceased all relationship therewith. The children had been attending the Sunday school of the Methodist Episcopal Church. This team was calling from that church. The workers had heard me, when giving instructions, emphatically request that they respect the other person's religious background. After they had been visiting a few moments, the German mother said: "I am worried about my children. They are old enough to be in classes leading to confirmation. I do not, however, wish to send them to the Lutheran Church here; the services are all held in the German language. I do not want my children to attend a church where the services are all in German."

The German worker said to this mother: "Why not send them over to our church and have them confirmed?"

She answered: "Oh! you do not confirm in your church."

"Yes, we do," the German worker replied. "We do not call it confirmation, but it is the same thing. We baptise children, if they have not been baptised before; we have them come to the altar and consecrate their lives to Jesus and His work in the world; we put them into instruction classes."

The German mother then said: "O, dats so goot—you may have my children."

This team of workers remembered that I had said never to take the promise of a second party, but always to see him themselves. So the worker said to the mother: "But, don't you think we should see the children?"

"O, no," she replied, "you may have my children"—and, as the workers were leaving the door, the mother continued: "If you don't mind, father and I would like to come over and join your church also."

Do you see what had happened? These workers had discovered a family that used to be in close relationship with a church, but that had severed the relationship and was not getting the Christian nurture that every family needs. The visitors had entered appreciatively into the religious background of this family; they had even used the religious vocabulary with which this German mother was acquainted. They had re-established their relationship with the Christian Church. Only God in Heaven knows what that will mean to posterity!

Another assumption that we make is that people are basically, universally, instinctively religious. It is very helpful when one is attempting to get a layman to do this work to call his attention to this fact. Oftentimes men say: "I could not do that—that is not in my line"; and really what they have in their mind is that it would be abrupt and out of

place to go into a man's home or his private office
and introduce a subject of conversation which is
absolutely foreign to the man's mind. The thing
that they are overlooking is that all men are interested in religion. It is the chief interest in life.
There are men who talk loudly upon the street and
would lead you to believe that they have no respect
for the Church and no confidence in its religious
program for the world. These same men, when
you get them in their own homes and ask them
some direct questions about their own personal
religious responsibility in the community, commence to reveal aspirations and hunger that you
never dreamed were in their minds and hearts.

One day in Burlington, Vermont—in the midst
of a wonderful single church campaign where we
won three hundred and nine individuals to a Christian decision in five days—we met a man. He was
the owner of a theatre. After we had announced
the purpose of our visit and had been talking for
a few moments, he asked: " Have you seen
Mr. A.? "

" No," I said. " Who is Mr. A.? "

" He is a friend of mine—a merchant," he
replied.

" Well," I said, " we will be glad to see Mr. A.
But just now we are interested in talking to you
about the Christian life and about your local religious responsibility."

" Go and see Mr. A., and if you get any-

where with him, come back and see me," he
returned.

I saw that it would be best to do as he suggested,
although I was quite sure that it was his strategy
to send us to a man whom *he* thought it was impossible for us to win. After we left his place of business, I said to Dr. Mark Kelly, pastor of the church
in Burlington: " Who is Mr. A.? "

" Oh," he answered, " he is a ' hard nut.' Now,
do not misunderstand me. He is highly respected
in the community and a good man; but it would be
absolutely useless to talk to him about making a
definite Christian decision."

" Well," I said, " let us see him."

" I think it will be a waste of time," he replied.

" We have been working pretty hard," I answered. " Let's take a vacation and go down and
see him."

When we arrived at the store, the clerk at the
counter told us Mr. A. was in the private
room. We asked if we might go back there
and see him, and were told we might. As we
entered the room, I said: " You're Mr. A., I
understand. You know Dr. Kelly, of course; he
is the pastor of the church up here. My name is
Kernahan. We have come to you to talk about the
Christian life, about church membership, and about
your religious responsibility in your community.
We would like to visit with you about what it
would mean if you would invest your personality

in the church here. Of course, you know, Mr.
A., that the Christian Church is like every other
human institution; speaking from the human
standpoint, it is the combined strength of the personalities that are invested in it. You, undoubtedly, want a Christian environment in which to
live; you wouldn't live where there were no public
schools."

"No," he replied.

"Well," I continued, "the public school is the
product of the Christian Church. You wouldn't
live where there was no system of jurisprudence."

Again he replied, "No."

"Well," I continued, "many of the protective
features of our system of jurisprudence, as we
have it now, have been fostered and nurtured in the
heart of the Christian Church. You would not live
in a community where there was no place for the
religious education of the children."

Again our friend answered in the negative.

"The Church is the only institution that furnishes that type of education," I went on. I had
already discovered that the general assumption of
the community that Mr. A. was *not* interested in
religion, was *false*.

I then asked him a number of direct questions.
"Do you receive Jesus Christ as your Saviour,
and confess Him as your Lord and Master?" I
asked him.

"Why," he said, pointing to an emblem on the

lapel of his coat, " Mr. Kernahan, I could not be a member of this organization if I did not believe that."

" I rather thought that you believed it," I said. " But I wondered just how personal your belief was. Have you just believed in a rather general way that Jesus Christ is your Saviour? Have you just, in a general way, confessed Him as your Lord and Master? If that be true, Mr. A., I am here, today, to appeal to you that you crystallize those general beliefs into a personal attitude and decision. Do you accept and profess the Christian faith as contained in the New Testament of our Lord Jesus Christ?"

" Why, yes. That's prerequisite to membership in the organization represented by this emblem."

" Yes, I know it is," I said, " because I, too, belong to that fraternity. But, the question is— just how personal have you made this profession of belief in the Christian faith? Do you believe that Jesus was right when He taught that God was a loving, Heavenly Father? Do you believe that Jesus was correct when He said that we live forever? Are you persuaded that Jesus was right when He taught that a human life is the most valuable thing in the world? You will remember that is told us in the fifteenth chapter of St. Luke's Gospel, in the story told of the shepherd who left the ninety-and-nine in the pasture and went out to look for the one that was lost."

Mr. A.'s attitude, as I discovered after I had questioned him upon these two matters, indicated that he had no question as to the legitimacy of this appeal. Then I said, " My friend, if you actually believe these things, I am sure that you will agree with me that it is necessary to have a church. You cannot perpetuate or promote anything unless it is organised. Now that's just where the local church comes in. If you are willing in a definite, positive manner to receive Jesus Christ as your Saviour, and to receive the Christian faith as taught in the New Testament, then it is your inevitable responsibility that you invest your personality in a church."

" I will think it over," was his answer.

Now, nine times out of every ten, when a man says he will " think it over," he is just dodging the issue. In as large a percentage of cases as I have here mentioned, he has been thinking it over more or less all his life. This is the biggest obstacle we meet in our work—not merely a spiritual laziness, but a psychological difficulty which gets in the way of an immediate decision. We do not need to persuade people that the Christian teachings are true,—ninety-five per cent. of them believe that— half as much as we need to persuade them to act on the thing that they already believe.

" All right, Mr. A.," I replied, " if you want to think it over, let's think it over together right now. Have you any problems, have you any

unbelief, have you any sinful practices? Is there
any obstacle in the way?" I discovered by these
questions, and others of like nature, that this man's
difficulty was procrastination. So I said to him,
"Mr. A., *today* is the *day* to make your decision!" This man who had been spoken of as
a "hard nut," insofar as a religious appeal was
concerned, commenced to show a good deal of
emotion and I saw that my opportunity had come.
"Mr. A.," I said, "if I could promise you that
if you were to make your decision today, we
could win at least six other men in Burlington
before the close of our work this week, would that
be any consideration to you?"

He turned toward me, reached out his hand and
said, "If you could assure me, Mr. Kernahan, that
my decision for Christ would win one person in
Burlington to a like decision, I would make it this
moment."

"Mr. A.," I replied, "I am safe in assuring you that if you will make your decision today,
we *will* win at least one other man, and possibly
several."

"I'll do it, then," he said. He signed his name
upon our "Record of Decision" card. We shook
hands, had a word of prayer, and once more it was
demonstrated that man everywhere is basically,
instinctively religious.

We could multiply this illustration by hundreds.
It is scarcely necessary. When we go with the

realisation that folks are thanking God that we came, that we feed an immense hunger, that we uncover and develop deep and sacred aspirations —then we can go out with a conviction and come back with tremendous results.

III

THE NEED OF A NEW METHOD OF EVANGELISM

THERE is a great need of a new method of evangelism in which the laymen can play a larger part. The method that I suggest is new to us, but not to Jesus. We have always talked about it—we have never tried it. It must be based upon a passionate fondness for mankind and a holy love for Jesus. We must set this method up at the foot of the Cross, for that is the only place where sufficient dynamic can be received to enable us to succeed. "At the foot of the Cross," says Sir Oliver Lodge, "there has been a perennial experience of relief and renovation. Ours is not a creed, it is a passion. Men in every age have died for it. In every land where its tale is told and with every new sun that dawns, drunkards may be found whom it has made sober, thieves whom it has taught to be honest, harlots whom it has lifted up to chastity, selfish men who, touched by its preaching, live by a great law of self-sacrifice. It is the root whence blossom great heroisms and charities. All human sorrows hide in His wounds. All human self-denials lean on His Cross."

It is here that every sincere layman, as well as ordained minister, may receive such a passionate fondness for people and such an appreciation of Jesus' spiritual power that he can become as powerful as any immediate disciple of Jesus ever was. Jesus said, " He that hath seen me hath seen the Father." Dr. Charles L. Goodell says, " In His own person He brought a spiritual power and dynamic which broke up the old order of the pagan world and founded a system based upon an uncalculating and overwhelming love. He mastered men and events, and broke into the leaden night with a blazing passion that was volcanic and irreristible. He broke up the order of His time to the breaking of His own heart." And Forsythe says, " He was an austere man, a severe critic, a born fighter, of choleric wrath and fiery scorn, so that the people thought He was Elijah or the Baptist. Yet He was gentle to the last degree, especially to those ignorant and out of the way. Clear, calm, determined and sure of His mark, He was the next hour roused to such impulsive passion as if He were beside Himself. But if He let Himself go, He always knew where He was going. He poured out His soul unto God and unto death and He was the friend of publicans and sinners."

If we found our new method at the foot of the Cross, these two indispensable possessions will be ours, namely, a passionate fondness for mankind, and a graphic appreciation of Jesus' spiritual power.

When we realise that Jesus said that we could do
greater things than these—referring to some things
that He and His immediate disciples had done—
then we are fired with an enthusiasm to try. As
we look out into the world, we understand better,
as our experience broadens, just what Jesus meant.
He meant that the world would be better prepared
in our day than in His to respond to the teaching
and preaching of good men who looked, and lived,
and worked, and loved like Jesus. There is now a
spiritual content in the world that did not exist
when He walked upon the earth. His spirit has
energised every race of people on earth. His name
is not strange! Where once there was violent
antagonism to His leadership, there is now admira-
tion. Where once there was misunderstanding,
there is now a partial recognition of His Saviourhood. Where once there was gross ignorance as to
His spiritual ability and transcending qualities in
general, there is now an increasing and ever ex-
panding spiritual literacy.

This new method must grow up within a congregation. It must not be imported. Responsibility
can not be shifted. We have had far too many
spiritual tragedies where congregations have attempted to place the entire responsibility for the
saving of their constituency upon the heart of their
pastor or upon some one else brought in from the
outside. Jesus can not fully nurture those who
are converted, unless the people into whose con-

gregation these individuals come, know something of the spiritual travail through which they came.

Now, as to the method. We are safe to follow Jesus here. He sent His disciples out two by two to visit, to do deeds of love, and to deliver messages of spiritual promise. Think of the Seventy, for instance. These men obeyed Jesus. They went out willing to use their lips to speak His message, and their hands to do His work of love. They came back so hilariously happy because of the things they had seen accomplished that they said, " Even the evil spirits are subject unto us." We have every right to conclude that we are sent just as these early disciples were. We have the same authority, we have the same commission. We will have greater success. The harvest is ripe.

The difference between this method and the method of mass evangelism lies in the fact that the laymen become the evangelists together with the pastors. The old method was liable to be the appeal of one man. Jesus could not possibly make a complete evangelistic appeal to a whole community through one man.

There is a difference in personality. Some are compatible, some are incompatible. There is a difference of experience and education in any community. We must be prepared for all types of personality, all degrees of experience and education, if we are to make a comprehensive evangelistic appeal to the unsaved portion of our constituency.

Too often the professional evangelist brought in to lead a campaign of mass evangelism, is reactionary in his theological outlook. Oftentimes he is eccentric, and his eccentricities are exaggerated for publicity purposes. Oftentimes he is a past master in the creating and directing of a dangerous mob psychology. Often the people who are won by this method are won to a certain theological interpretation of the Bible, which is mechanical and out of date. When the evangelist leaves, these people become discouraged and fall away. Every pastor knows that there is great danger of a bad aftermath when this method is used.

Another method is needed, not only actually to have a comprehensive evangelistic appeal, but in order to answer the greatest hunger of our laymen. Since the first time that a layman came to a definite realisation of his immediate relationship to Jesus and the Father, he has wanted to win others to this same consecrated relationship. Give him the opportunity, furnish him the instructions, place in his hands the names of friends and neighbours to whom to go, tell him that Jesus goes with him, and do this all at the foot of the Cross, and straightway he will come back with the wonderful story that five, ten, fifteen people have made their decision for Christ at his solicitation.

I do not wish to be unduly critical, but the very logic of our present situation drives us, if we are to be practical, to this new method. I have followed carefully the work of evangelists, who once were successful, for the last four years, and it is very evident that mass evangelism has largely served its day in many sections of the country. Let us accept without reservation the fact that hundreds of members in a church will do far more towards evangelism in any community by going out in teams of two and visiting in the most courteous, direct, and persuasive manner with their friends and neighbours about the claims of Christ upon life and the demands of present day Christian citizenship, than any one man can possibly do by attempting to get decisions for Christ in a public service.

IV

WHAT WAS JESUS' METHOD?

A PERSON is supremely fortunate when he discovers Jesus' way of doing anything. This is especially true in the field of evangelism. Our immediate concern here is, how did Jesus try to win His followers? One does not read very long in the New Testament before he comes to the conclusion that Jesus never held a series of meetings for the purpose of winning His followers. He preached, and no man will ever preach like Jesus did, but when it came to the definite task of winning His followers, He went to them or called them to Him. He talked with them on the road, when He walked, or while He rested at the well, or in some other homely place. You will remember that when Jesus was baptised, the man who baptised him said, " Behold the Lamb of God." There were some people who overheard this announcement, and one man by the name of Andrew came to Jesus. Jesus had an interview with Andrew and immediately, in the most natural way in the world, Andrew became a disciple of Jesus.

There is something so simple, so beautiful about

Jesus' contact. Andrew was at once filled with a passion to win others. He could think of no one on earth that he would rather bring to Jesus than his own brother, so he went at once to his tempestuous brother Peter and brought him to Jesus. Jesus did not ask a number of dogmatic questions. He interpreted Peter to himself, and during that conversation, Peter, one of the most interesting characters of the New Testament, was won to Christian discipleship.

Jesus was out walking one day and He saw a man. He called to him, " Follow Me," and a man by the name of Philip came at once to Jesus' side. He had not been long in contact with the spirit of Jesus when he, like Andrew, said to himself, " Now, whom can I bring to Christ?" He thought how wonderful it would be for his brother Nathanael to become acquainted with Jesus, so he proceeded at once to get his brother. There is just a little interesting side light here on human nature. When he met Nathanael he told him about Jesus and told him whence He came; and Nathanael revealed one of the age-long human tendencies when he said, " Why, how could it be that a man such as you say Jesus is could come from the place He did?" However, Philip was so sure that he had met one who had spiritual dynamic enough to make life triumphant that he persisted in his entreaty, and Nathanael consented to meet Jesus. Jesus saw him coming and the story that is told of their introduction is exceedingly interesting. Jesus told him that he was without guile. Nathanael immediately accepted Jesus' spiritual dictatorship, and became His obedient friend and loving servant.

I like to think of another man whom Jesus interviewed, who had the same handicap that I have —whenever he wanted to see anything, he had to stand up on something. He came hurrying down to see Jesus. The people were all tiptoeing to look upon the beautiful face of the Master and to hear His musical voice, and to be thrilled with His message of love. This man was all puffed up with dignity because he had been elected to a position of public trust. He forgot all about his dignity and tried to look over the folks into the face of Jesus, but found that it was impossible; so he ran down the road ahead of Jesus, climbed up into a sycamore tree, and looked down to see Jesus as He passed. Now notice how natural our Divine Example was here. He looked up into the face of Zacchæus and said, "Come down, Zacchæus, I want to go home and dine with you." On their way home, Jesus talked to him about the program of the Kingdom of God.

Zacchæus was so thrilled and charmed by the altruistic purpose of the heart of Christ that he said, "I'll tell you what I'll do, Jesus, I'll give fifty per cent. of all the goods I possess to works of charity." This is a good proof of conversion. I have known some folks who lived in the Church all of their lives and you could not convince them, to save your soul, that they should give ten per cent. to Christian work.

Jesus seemed to anticipate the fact that people would be rather hesitant to adopt His method of evangelism, and the history of the Christian Church proves that His anticipation was correct. One of the reactions that one meets in this work is the growing astonishment that comes as one notes the phenomenal success that many sincere laymen have in this work, when one remembers that for over nineteen hundred years we have almost entirely forsaken Jesus' method of evangelism.

As though He were to say one more final and emphatic word upon this subject, He has a conversation one day with a woman at a well. He is sitting upon the well platform and a woman comes to draw water. He engages her in conversation and, using the figure of the water as a symbol of spiritual life, He speaks of "Living Water." He tells her all about her past life. She admits that His story is true. She marvels at His courtesy and sympathy. He turns her attention from the past to the future. She grasps the opportunity of redemption. She hurries at once back to the village and persuades her friends and neighbours, who knew all about her bad past, to come and meet her Saviour. This story proves beyond any doubt that any person who is sincere can do this work. All that a person needs is a capacity for friendship and

an acquaintanceship with Christ to be able to visit
with others in a winning manner about Jesus'
personality and Saviourhood.

Send a number of laymen, two by two, out into
any community to visit about Jesus with the people
for whom your church is responsible, and there will
be others like Andrew, Peter, Philip, Nathanael,
Zacchæus and the Woman at the Well, who will
accept the invitation to meet Jesus. When once
they have met Jesus, it will be the most simple and
natural thing in the world for them to confess their
faith in Him at some church altar, and to be received as members of the group of modern disciples. This was Jesus' method—it should be ours.
We must learn to capitalise the spiritual and psychological elements, just as a good salesman does,
but for the purpose of the presentation of the
Christian religion.

II

HOW TO ORGANIZE

V

PREPARATORY WORK

WORK in the field of evangelism has suffered for lack of careful organisation. Sometimes we have emphasised the absolute necessity of the presence of the Holy Spirit in an enterprise of this kind, with an inference that the Holy Spirit would not work in an organised and systematic way. Some churches have given the impression that they thought the Holy Spirit was not interested in the work of evangelism at any other time than in the winter. I have heard people say, " We will wait until the meetings next winter." I have heard pastors say, " I am anticipating that Mr. A. will make his decision when the meetings come on." If I understand the Holy Spirit, my idea is that He would instruct us that *every* week in the year is acceptable to Him; that He comes whenever people receive Him. Let us always remember that the Holy Spirit has seemed to be present with greater power at certain seasons than at others, simply because we prepared ourselves better these times to receive Him.

This fact points to the necessity of preparatory work. We must prepare ourselves, not only in spiritual fervour, but also in a carefully outlined program of procedure. The first part of the preparatory work is very important. John Stuart Blackie says: "The Early Church worked by a fervid moral contagion, not by the suasion of cool argument. The Christian method of conversion, not by logical arguments, but by moral contagion and the effusion of the Holy Ghost, has with the masses of mankind always proved itself the most effective." We should prepare ourselves by prayer and by the reading of spiritual conquest, both in the Bible and in books which record great spiritual achievements. We must irradiate religious earnestness and contagious enthusiasm. This type of spiritual mood becomes the dynamic in our work. We must, however, be so well organised that the spiritual energy that we exert will be directed to the proper places of need, or we will expend our physical strength and spiritual suasion to little effect. Therefore, we make the following suggestions:

1. The pastor should set apart one week for intensive work. He should have all-the-year-around evangelism—and he can have it; but he must first have a demonstration of what Christ can do through a number of laymen in this method. Therefore, he should have a date marked on his church calendar for a one week Intensive Visitation Evangelistic Campaign.

2. The pastor should make a very careful Re-

sponsibility Roll. This list should carry the names of every man, woman, boy, and girl in the community for whose religious nurture his church is responsible. This list should be complete; no one should be missed. Then these names should be transcribed upon a Prospect Card, giving the nature of the person's relations to the church, and any other information that will assist those who call upon him.

3. The pastor should secure just as large a number of laymen as he possibly can to do the calling. The best way to enroll them as workers is to go to them privately and get their signatures upon a Visitation Committee Agreement Card. He can enlist a great many people in this work by assuring them that wherever the laymen have attempted to do this service, they have had phenomenal success; that, for instance, one director in campaigns that resulted in the winning of over ten thousand people found, when the results were averaged, that each team of two laymen had won fourteen new people; that he, the pastor, understands that they feel as if they cannot do it, but if they will only try, he will release them if they should find they are not succeeding. The pastor will never have to release a person.

These workers should designate exactly the amount of time that they will give. We find that it is much better to get them to promise to work during all the periods set aside in one week, than

to allow them to spread their periods of work over
a longer length of time. Have them sign for Sunday afternoon, and every evening of the week with
the exception of Saturday.

4. The pastor should make arrangements for a
workers' supper at 6:00 or 6:15 every evening of
the "intensive." This supper is very essential.
You will find that the workers will be much more
regular and punctual when a supper is served
than they would be if they had to get their supper at home first. A great many interruptions are
avoided. Then there is virtue in the fact that
when the workers eat together, they have the opportunity to talk about the work. We will say,
for instance, that two men are sitting side by side
at the table. Mr. A. failed last night to win anybody. Mr. B. won four. Mr. B. is so enthusiastic
about his success that he becomes a veritable fountain of inspiration for Mr. A. Mr. A. goes out
from the supper with a great deal more courage
than he would have had if he had eaten at home
and thought about last night's failure. The Prospect Cards which were used the night before are
turned in while the people are eating. The new
assignments for that evening's work are made the
moment the supper is finished. Several of the
workers give their reports. They tell of their experiences, and of the problems that they have met.
The director seizes this opportunity to emphasise
the instructions that are needed to meet the situ-

ations that are revealed. Immediately at the close of his address, which must be condensed and literally saturated with inspiration, the group engages in prayer, and at the conclusion of the prayer, they go to work at once.

5. The pastor should ask all those whom he secures as workers to give special time in prayer in preparation for this enterprise. It is best to ask them privately. He should ask any wife whose husband is on the prospect list, and also any husband whose wife is on the prospect list, and likewise any member of the family who is interested in any other member of the family becoming a Christian, to pray for that person. He should warn them, however, not to speak to that person about the matter until the name is assigned unless they are impressed with the fact that the Holy Spirit leads them to do so.

6. The pastor should prepare two classes of instruction for church membership. This schedule of work should be carefully outlined, the teacher secured, and everything made ready to place these new members in classes the minute that they make their confession of Christ at the altar. The way in which these people are received into the church is entirely in the hands of the pastor—the director has nothing to say about that. He suggests, however, that the young people be given a thorough course of training in what it means to be a Christian citizen today; what it means to be a member

of any Christian church. He suggests that the older ones, who have not had a Sunday School and church background, either be given instruction in a class that meets at a regularly appointed time, or be given an outline for reading. I would have a series of religious educational and cultural addresses a few weeks after the " intensive."

If this preparatory work is done carefully, and sensitiveness to the leadership of the Holy Spirit is magnified, any church anywhere on earth may have a Pentecost. A passion for the work and organisation of the work are both absolutely essential.

VI

WHEN AND HOW TO LAUNCH

THE method of Visitation Evangelism may be launched the moment the preparatory work is done. The season of the year is immaterial. The only time that we must avoid is the summer vacation period, which takes a large percentage of the people out of the community, or brings in a large number who are to be cared for in the homes of the people upon whom we would call. But there are ten months of the year which can be used for this work. There are no exceptions to this statement. The weather is a consideration, but from the opposite point of view of the old method. The worse the weather, the better the chances of success; people are more liable to be home when it is raining; those who are calling will be able to find them.

After the preparatory work has been carefully done, the campaign should be launched—on a Sunday. It is well to have a director; in fact, I should not advise any church to launch its first campaign without some minister who has one or more week's experience in this work. A man who is acquainted with technique of the work gains confidence, speaks with authority and proceeds with an assurance which are invaluable to those who have never done this work before. This director should visit the various departments of the Sunday School, speak about ten minutes in each department, and tell in the clearest and most direct manner just what is to be done that week. He should attempt to win co-operation in these departments. At the regular morning preaching hour, he should preach a sermon in which he magnifies the fact that Jesus can save this world for the Kingdom of God just the minute that the laymen will volunteer to carry the message. The laymen should be led to see that the great unused resource of the church is the combined personality of its laity. At 2:30 in the afternoon he should meet the workers. He should go over in the most careful manner the background, technique, and appeals of Visitation Evangelism. That we may be clear here, I will cover these three things briefly.

1. The background of the method. We have been driven to attempt a new method because we are in a new day of evangelism. Mass evangelism has very largely served its day and is gone, or is going. Visitation evangelism is in accordance with Jesus' own work. He won His followers by personal contact; His immediate disciples won folks by the personal contact method. The members of the early church extended the work of the church and the Kingdom of God by personal inter-

view. The laymen who will do this work today will have amazing results. One director of this work has directed laymen who have won in ten months of work over ten thousand people to decisions for Christ and for church membership.

2. Technique. The workers should be instructed to be direct, courteous, and persistent. The moment they meet a person at the door, they should announce their errand in some such manner as this, " Our church has set aside a week in which we are attempting to call upon every man, woman, boy, and girl in this community who has any connection with our church and who, so far as we know, has never made a decision for Christ." Then, after getting into the home (always get in: if a person does not invite you in, say, " We'll only take a few moments of your time, may we please come in and go over the matter with you?") ask him, " Have you ever been a member of any Christian church? " It will depend upon the person's answer as to how the workers will proceed. If the person says he was a member of such-and-such a church in some other place, then it will be a good thing to say something like this, " Give us the information and our pastor will send for your church-letter." Never say, " Don't you think you should send for your letter? " " When will you let us get your letter? " or " How soon may the pastor send for your letter? " Such questions suggest that there are two sides to the matter of church transfer. There is

only one side. A person has no right to live in one
community and belong to a church in some other
place—it is impossible to send one's personality by
proxy. He is either functioning for Christ and
the Church in the place where he lives, or nowhere.
Put the matter in a constructive sentence like this,
" Give us the information and our pastor will send
for your letter."

It may be, however, that even when you put your
request in this form, the person will hesitate on
account of sentimental associations. He will tell
you that his mother and father were members of
that church for twenty years, that he met his wife
there, that they were married by the pastor, and
that their babies were baptised there. If he does
this, remind him that he was fortunate enough to
have a father and mother who were loyal enough
to their religious responsibility to assume their local
Christian and church relationship; that every
reason which argued that they should be careful
about their religious duties and privileges, also
argues that he and his wife should be definitely
related where they live. If you do not succeed at
this point on account of these sentimental associations, then do the rather severe thing of suggesting
to him that the pastor back there at the old church
will be glad to remove his membership from that
church to some other. This will probably be an
absolutely new consideration to the person. He
felt that they cherished his membership back there

in the old church, when as a matter of fact, any pastor feels that he is doing his friend the very best service by getting him related to the church in the community where he lives. This argument usually brings his permission to get the transfer.

On the other hand, we will suppose that the man says he has never been a member of any church. Then I would suggest proceeding by asking several direct questions to discover just what the man's attitude is toward Christ and Church. If you discover, as we do in numerous instances, that his attitude is friendly, insist, in a tactful, gracious manner, to get an immediate decision. My own method is to ask him if he is willing to accept Jesus Christ as his Saviour, and to confess Him as his Lord and Master; if he receives and professes the Christian faith as contained in the New Testament of our Lord Jesus Christ? I ask him whether he will be loyal to the Church and uphold it by his prayer, his presence, his gifts and his service? If he answers in the affirmative, then I indicate to him the fact that I would like to have him make this statement: that he accepts Jesus Christ as his personal Saviour and purposes, with His help, to live a Christian life and do all he can to help carry out His entire program; that he will unite with a church which he indicates as his choice and will present himself for membership at that church upon a definite Sunday. If I find that it is more difficult to win him than this description just given indicates, then I proceed to make one of several appeals.

3. Appeals.   There is the appeal to conscience. Every person on earth knows the difference between right and wrong.   A worker should take advantage of this fact.   If I were calling upon a father and were going to make the appeal to conscience, I would proceed somewhat after this fashion as indicated on an earlier page.   "You would not live in a community where there were no public schools if you could avoid it?"

The answer would always be, "No."

Then I would remind him that the public school was the product of the Christian Church.   "You would not live in a community where there was no system of jurisprudence?"

His answer again would be, "No."

Then I would suggest that the system of jurisprudence which we have has many protective features which have been fostered and nurtured in the Christian Church.   "You would not live where there was no opportunity to send your children to Sunday school?"

In most instances, his answer again would be, "No."

Then I would again remind him that the Sunday school is perpetuated by the gifts and leadership of the people in the church.   I would then directly and frankly impress him with the fact that he was demanding a certain kind of social environment,

which is in a real sense Christian, in which to rear
his children; that this demand made him mutually
responsible with every other person in the community who made a like demand; that just at
present he seemed to be assuming that somebody
else would carry his religious responsibility; that
that really was not the thing he would choose to
do when he realised that he was doing it. I would
call his attention to the fact that the only way to
perpetuate any institution is to invest personality
in it. I would ask him if he did not think it perfectly fair to expect him to put his life into the
Church if he desired the continuance of the kind
of an environment which he now demanded in the
community where he was building his home?

This presentation of Christian citizenship will
have a challenge in it that he never saw before.
He will realise that he has the opportunity to pour
his life and spiritual energy into the life of his
children, not only through the home, but through
every other institution in the community which he
needs to supplement the work of the home, if he
is to reach the highest goal that he has in mind for
his children. If I were talking to a mother, I
should make the same appeal. If I were talking to
a youth, I should attempt to persuade him that
he was not using his time and talents properly
and ask him if he were not preparing himself
for some really constructive and altruistic purpose in the world. Now this appeal in either

instance is an appeal to conscience—as to whether the person is using his physical strength, his mental ability, and the influence of his personality for the purpose that God intended—as to whether he is really fair to himself, to others, and to his Heavenly Father.

The second appeal is the appeal for a Christian home. This is a tender and beautiful appeal. I never direct a campaign without having a number of experiences with this method of approach which would furnish memories that would recompense me for a lifetime of service. I meet parents in their homes and ask them such a question as this: " Of course you want to have a Christian home? " If you have the children gathered around you, if perhaps you have some fine little laddie on your knee, ask father and mother if it be not true that they would do anything on earth that was possible and legitimate to secure the spiritual and moral standards of the laddie? Remind them, too, that God gives the fingers of mothers and fathers a power to paint into the background of the child's life, a beauty superior to any other beauty on earth.

Whenever I call where there are children who have not made their Christian decision, I start with them. The question arises here, of course, as to at what age a child should consider this matter? At one time I had a minimum age, but my own children violated it. When I first enrolled in the academy, I remember that the first teachers in child psychology that there were in that day, agreed that the age of accountability was sixteen years. Before I finished college, they had decided that it was twelve years. Recently they have decided that the age of choice, for that is what they call it now, is eleven years. The minimum age that I used to observe in this work was twelve years, but my own little laddie came home from church two consecutive Sundays crying and saying to his mother, " I want to be a Christian, Mamma."

His mother, thank God, knew how Christ had declared the children were Christians. She said, " Earl, my boy, you are a Christian, but do you mean that you want to go forward in the church and in that way tell everybody that you want to continue to be a friend of Jesus; that you want Him to go with you all through the years of your life as your Companion?"

" Yes, Mamma," he replied.

The next Sunday when I gave the opportunity for any one who desired to confess his faith in Christ and join the church to come forward, Earl came down the aisle. As he came toward the altar, the thought occurred to me that it was really God's work; that there is no time in all the life of a person when it is quite so wise for him to choose Jesus' companionship as it is at that first moment when he chooses Jesus to be his friend forever—just at that moment he is old enough to become a Christian by his own choice. Up to that minute he is a

Christian through the nurture of Christian environment and by virtue of the fact that every child on earth is a Christian. Therefore, I always begin my appeal with the children, and after having won the children, I then proceed to win the parents.

I once directed a Visitation Evangelism campaign in St. Paul's Methodist Episcopal Church at Cedar Rapids, Iowa. One night after the workers' supper, a young man came hurrying to me and said, " Dr. Kernahan, please give this evening to me."

" Paul," I said, " I am afraid that Dr. Jayne has already assigned me to some one else. You go over and ask Dr. Jayne." Dr. Jayne told him that I was to work that evening with Mr. A. L. Killian, one of the outstanding merchants of the city. Then I said, " You ask Mr. Killian, Paul, if I can give you thirty minutes and we will make that one call that you mentioned especially."

" Why, surely, Paul," Mr. Killian said; " you and Mr. Kernahan jump into my car and I will take you over."

We had no sooner arrived in the home where Paul directed us than the father came in and said, " Paul, my answer tonight is exactly the same as it was last night and the night before." I then discovered that Paul had laid siege to that home; this made three calls in three consecutive nights. If I had known that Paul had called on the two previous nights, I would have advised him to wait a day or so before he made another call; but we were there and we had met a flat refusal. (This is about the worst situation that you can meet in this work.) Fortunately a boy about nineteen years of age came in the front door, and just at the same time the mother, with a girl about twelve years of age and a boy of fifteen came in from the dining room.

This was exceedingly encouraging to me. I felt that now we could get around and past the father's refusal. I turned to the older boy. Usually I start with the youngest child, but for some reason which I am not now able to explain, I commenced with the older boy. I said to him, "You want to be a Christian."

"Yes, I do," he answered.

"If I remember correctly," I continued, "when I was a young man of your age, I thought that to be a Christian meant to be willing to consecrate my body, my mind, and all that I had to Christ and His service. I felt that it was necessary to learn all that I could about Jesus and to be just as much like Him as I possibly could. Are you willing to do that?"

"Yes, I am!" he answered emphatically.

"Can you answer these questions?" I asked him. I then repeated to him the three questions which we ask people who are being received into our church: "Do you receive Jesus Christ as your Saviour and confess Him as your Lord and Master? Do you receive and profess the Christian faith as taught in the New Testament of our Lord

Jesus Christ? Will you be loyal to the church and uphold it by your prayer, your presence, your gifts and your service?"

He had answered each question in the affirmative. We clasped hands, bowed our heads and had a word of prayer.

Then I turned to the boy fifteen years of age and had a very similar conversation with him. He was easily won. Then I talked to the little girl twelve years of age, and explained the questions in her own language. She, of course, was willing to be a Christian. Then I directed my appeal to the mother. She was a typical mother; she could not resist the pull of the fact that her children were ready to take their places in the Church and grow into splendid Christian citizens. She made her decision.

Then I turned to the father and said, " Dad, here is your family. If you make your decision for Christ while your oldest boy is at home, you will have to do it pretty soon, for if he does as most sons do, he will be gone from home in two or three years; and you wouldn't let him go away from home with the thought that Dad refused to make his Christian decision when he was at home and wanted him to come at the same time that he made his decision. You wouldn't send him away like that. And, here is your boy fifteen years of age. You know how vital it is to his Christian growth that he have your example. No person can take your place. He has a right to expect you to stand with him at the altar and swear your allegiance to Jesus Christ, who helps every good man in the business of growing big souls in his children. Here is your little girl. How fortunate it is that she desires to make her choice of Christ and His leadership just now when she is young. You, together with mother here, are giving yourselves for this little girl and her brothers, whom you want to succeed to the very highest degree in this noble undertaking. Your little girl has a right to expect her father to choose her Christ as his Lord."

The big railroad man stood up, showed a good deal of emotion, and said he would do anything in the world for his children.

" Then be a Christian for their sakes," I said.

He said, " I will." This is the appeal for a Christian home.

I told this story once at Morningside College, Sioux City, Iowa, and one of the students said, " Mr. Kernahan, how deep does a decision like that go when a parent makes his decision for his children's sake? "

" If I understand the human heart at all, it goes about as deep as anything in all his experience," I answered. " Many parents will make their decision for the Christian life for the sake of their children who would not do it for their own sakes because of reticence and other similar obstructions."

The third appeal is for service. This is directly

in keeping with the spirit of today. We do not
have much respect for a man's testimony of Christian loyalty and devotion unless that man is doing
something for society and for God. Of course
there is one exception. There are some people who
are physically disabled, old and infirm, who have
rich Christian experiences and cannot work, but
these are exceptions. To be able to convince people
that they can take whatever personal ability God
has given them and use it for the sake of society, is
necessary. This appeal succeeds with people of
wealth, influence, and strong personality. It also
succeeds with youth.

On one occasion we went to call upon a man in
a large office building in a great city. He was
rich. We had some difficulty in getting to his
private office, but finally we were ushered into his
presence. "What do you want?" he said.

"We have come to talk to you about the Christian life," I replied—"about the Christian Church,
and about the necessity of a man of your standing
and ability investing his personality in it."

"This is a very busy morning," he returned.
"I am negotiating a loan of a million and-a-half
dollars to the corporation across the street here that
is constructing the new building on the opposite
corner."

"Give us ten minutes of your time, please," I
answered.

"Go ahead," he said.

In the next ten minutes we told him about everything we could about colleges, hospitals, and institutions of all kinds and descriptions. We showed him that for the first time in the history of organised Christianity the Church was attempting to eliminate duplication of work; that an actual assigning of the various areas of the earth's surface was being undertaken so that no two churches would be working in the same place and overlapping work. We did all we could to show him that the Church needed Christian statesmanship; that no man had a right to use his own abilities for his own interests alone. I held my watch in my hand and noticed that we were within one minute of the expiration of the ten-minute limit. I used that one minute in the most impassioned appeal that I knew how to make; saying that I did not believe that any man, who had a strong enough personality to be employed by six different corporations, had any right to sell his personality and his managerial powers to secular corporations alone, and neglect his responsibility to the Church, which must be perpetuated and become prosperous by the investment of the same kind of personality and leadership as these other organisations. The last minute slipped away, and I said, " Our ten minutes are gone; I thank you for your time. We expect that you will give this matter careful consideration."

" I will call you up in a couple of days," he answered.

This was very encouraging, for this man had an executive type of mind, and I knew that he would not call us up unless he felt that he would have something to say after the exercise of careful consideration.

On Thursday evening after the workers' supper the telephone bell rang. I answered it. It was this wealthy man, and he said, "Is this Mr. Kernahan?"

I answered that it was.

"I am Mr. So-and-so," he went on. "Will you please come over?"

"I will come at once," I replied.

I do not know when I had ever wanted so much to win a person to the Christian life. We hurried over to his home and he received us graciously.

"I have thought the matter over about which we were talking the other day," he said, "and if the minister will receive me into the church, I will be there a week from Sunday morning to make my confession of faith, as you suggested, and be received into church membership." I was so glad over this decision that I could scarcely control my feelings. Then he called his wife. She came into the parlour, a beautiful woman, undoubtedly a woman of great influence, and he said, "Mary, I have told these gentlemen that I am ready to make my confession of faith in Christ and be received into church membership. What do you think about it?"

"Oh, you know what I think about it," she answered; "I have wanted to do this for years."

"Then will you come with me a week from Sunday morning?" the husband asked.

"Of course I will," the wife replied. "There isn't anything that you could ask me to do that I would do more gladly."

The man then called his boy Carl. A big, athletic boy, possibly twenty years of age, came into the room. Turning to him the father said, "Carl, will you forgive me?"

"What on earth are you talking about, Dad?" replied the boy.

"I haven't given you the religious instruction and training I should," his father answered. "I have not given you the example in church attendance that I should. Will you forgive me?" Now, remember, this was the man who a few days before did not think that he had time to talk with us.

Carl said, "Why, of course, Dad, I will forgive you."

"Well, then, Carl," the father said, "will you come with Mother and myself to the church a week from Sunday morning and there make your confession of faith and be received into church membership?"

The big fellow shot out his hand and gripped his father's hand and said, "Dad, I will be with you!" It was the appeal for service that had attracted interest and convicted this father. The father had invited all the members of the family to become Christians, and they had accepted his invitation.

The fourth appeal is the one with which all pastors who have had any experience with revival services are well acquainted. It was about the only appeal that was made at one time in the history of evangelism. It is the exhortation to be prepared for the Hereafter, to develop capacity to enjoy Heaven, to be sure of the other world. The only place that we use this appeal now is where death has recently made the other world seem very near. I am not discussing the merits of this appeal; I am simply saying that the only place where it succeeds now is where Heaven seems very near because some loved one has taken up his residence there.

The very interesting fact about the method of Visitation Evangelism is that the difficulty of seasons and the interruptions of bad weather are eliminated. The campaign may be put on at any time with success assured. Any group of laymen who are led to fully appreciate the tremendous value of adapting their aggressive evangelistic work to this new day, who are given instructions in the technique of the work, and furnished with the sweeping instructions concerning the four outstanding appeals, will have phenomenal success.

VII

WORKERS' REPORTS

IN our last chapter we advised that the campaign be not launched without having the advantages of a director who had actually experienced one or more of these campaigns.

He sends the visitors out immediately after his address on Sunday afternoon. They have been assigned a number of people who are the most likely to make their decision. The sooner they get to their work after his last word of instruction, the better. We have often failed in personal evangelism in the Church because of our inability to get the workers actually to put into practice the things that have been told them in their instructions.

Now it is very important that these workers have the experience of winning a number to Christ before the Sunday evening meeting. They come back to the church on Sunday night with the glad news that five, or ten, or twenty, or fifty were won this afternoon. This news is the finest kind of publicity. It does not build up resistance, but it does give the workers enthusiasm, and at the same time brings a very gratifying response from the community outside of the church. At the Sunday evening service the workers are given some further assignments and instructed to report back at the Monday night workers' supper and conference. The workers bring their cards to the Monday night service with notations concerning their work upon the cards. If they have won the person, they write " WON " across the face of the card. If they failed to win the person, they write the reason why and make follow-up recommendations. If they feel that they can make further progress by a second call, they indicate that on the card. If, on the other hand, they are quite sure that some other team would have better success, they suggest that it would be well to re-assign the card.

The director looks these cards over while the teams are eating, and discovers what the particular situations are that have been met by the workers up to this time. He also discovers what visitors have had the best success. He chooses from three to five of these workers to make reports, instructing them to tell about their successes, and to relate the problems that they have met. The enthusiasm of those who have been especially successful becomes dynamic in the meetings. These reports must be made in two minutes. Brevity is of great importance in this workers' conference. The minute that these workers have finished their reports, the director should launch into his ten or twelve minute address, meeting the problems that the workers have discovered with the tersest and most direct answer. The spiritual situation is fully taken care of by the enthusiasm of the workers who have tasted that sublime experience of being actually instrumental in winning some person to the Christian life. A psychological situation is set up when the workers find the director answering the problems that they discovered in their work thus far. His instructions are inculcated into their very nature as they proceed to their work. They do not become stereotyped, for they have already done the work in their own way—they simply receive the information which they felt they needed so badly, and instead of the answers of the director being used in a memoriter way, they become a very part of the workers' mental and spiritual furnishings.

The fact that the workers are given definite assignments every evening and are expected to make a definite report the next evening, is of immense value in this work. It rescues evangelism from the vague, disorganised, hap-hazard method, where some lazy person has said that he did not feel that the Holy Spirit led him to go to his friend, and puts it upon the substantial basis where the Holy Spirit can actually be heard and is quite likely to be obeyed. The Kingdom of God will reap a harvest heretofore undreamed of, because of the fact that the unfathomable spiritual depths of the laity are directed to a definite purpose by this method.

VIII

INSTRUCTION OF THE WORKERS

MOST classes in personal evangelism that I have observed have met for a few weeks, have been instructed in the way to do the work, and then have never done it. There is a very obvious reason for this fact. The workers were given a number of questions and answers. They were given a number of Scriptural references. Certain inspirational subject-matter was read and discussed. They became more and more stereotyped as the classes proceeded. The answers that they had for the various questions that they anticipated would be asked, became a thing of memory rather than a passionate reaching out of the worker's own spirit for the one with whom he was talking. The person's personality was being covered up; he was becoming stiff and stilted. We proceed with the conviction that the biggest thing that a man has, so far as his human equipment is concerned, is his own personality; and when he goes out to work, he should go with the determination to be natural. God expects us to be natural. We are most persuasive when we are natural.

When the workers go out after the Sunday af-

ternoon meeting, they go with their hearts bare
for the task. They have been told that the best
way to succeed is to be themselves; to give just
whatever they have of intellectual and emotional
power to this one task, to discover themselves;
and then dedicate themselves to this business of
Jesus. Consequently, they win the confidence of
the people to whom they are talking. It is very
evident that there is no ulterior purpose. A rich
friendship often develops. The worker finds that
in winning his neighbour to himself, he has also
won him to Christ.

On Monday night we find that the workers have
discovered several peculiar situations. We find
that in answer to their invitation to become followers of Christ, people most always say: " I will
think it over." " We may move." " There are
too many hypocrites in the Church." " Can I not
be as good without becoming a member of the
church? " " I do not feel like it."

We instruct the workers to be very careful to
discover when a man says, " I will think it over,"
whether he is just trying to dodge the appeal, or
whether he really does desire time for further consideration. However, nine times out of ten when
we receive this answer, the person is simply attempting to postpone his decision. A large percentage of people *have* thought it over. What they
need is not further thought about it, but to be
persuaded to act upon the thing that they already

believe. If the person is really sincere in his wish for further consideration, then we instruct the workers to give him a kindly, direct, frank statement of what it is to be a Christian today, and make a date for a return call.

We instruct the workers to meet the answer, "We may move," in this manner: Suggest to that person that probably that is the main reason why he should make his Christian decision; that he should confess his faith in Christ among a group of people whom he knows and join the church in this community; and that the pastor will be delighted to transfer his membership to the new town or city to which he moves; that this will be a splendid way to become acquainted with the Christian people of the new community. I tell the workers to keep it in their minds that there are many families who are on the threshold of moving all the time.

When the workers meet the answer, "There are too many hypocrites in the Church," I tell them to admit frankly that there are; but to remind the person who says this that the Church is subject to the same weaknesses as any other human institution; that the question, however, that faces any particular person is not a responsibility for the inconsistency, weaknesses, and sins of some in the Church; but his own responsibility for his religious obligations. The question that faces *him* is whether religion is important to him, whether he believes in the reality of Christ, whether he should actually confess his faith in Jesus Christ as his Saviour, whether he can be true to Christ and stay outside of the institution that Jesus loves so much? For, even before the Church was organised, Jesus anticipated its organisation and spoke of the Church as His Bride. I think He used this term because it was the most affectionate term that He could use; and He has chosen the Church as the primary institution for the teaching and preaching of the Christian religion for over nineteen hundred years. Of course, it is impossible to wave away any person's responsibility by simply pointing to men and women inside of the Church who fail to measure up to their God-given privilege. I call their attention to the fact that in Jesus' first group of twelve, there was Judas; and that one of the beautiful things about Jesus' attitude then was that He did not become agitated, sour, and critical; He simply went on patiently serving mankind until Judas eliminated himself. We are not responsible for the other man's failure. We are responsible for our influence and for the perpetuation of the Christian Church, if we believe in the superiority of Jesus as a religious leader.

If I find that the visitors have met the answer, which is in the form of a question, " Can I not be good without joining the Church? " I make the following suggestions: This really is not the question that the person is facing at all. We are not particularly interested in just how good a person can be outside of the Church. There is one sure thing about it, however, that if a person is good outside of the Church, he should immediately thank the Church for his goodness. Every moral standard he has, has either been made and then lifted up by the Church, or else has been found and filled full of life and significance by it. His moral stamina to resist the evil forces and influences that attack every living being is undoubtedly the product of inheritance and teaching that the Church has provided for him. He should face frankly, then, the question as to whether he can really express his gratitude for what he has received without putting his life into the Church. He has received what he has of morality because others were willing to perpetuate a religious environment and the Christian Church. He surely should be willing and glad to pass on to posterity the things that he has received in the only possible way; that is by giving his influence and the push of his spirit to Christ's Church.

I also remind him that there is really something further to consider in the matter of one's decision. We should meet Christ's attitude in this matter. Usually Christ's attitude is accepted as authority by good people. What does He expect? How does He feel about the Church? Does He want the Church continued? Has He been able to use it in the past? Where have the reforms which have made the progress in the moral history of the human race been fostered and empowered? Does not Jesus refer to the Church as His Bride? I remind the person further that he can claim no freedom from obligation to the perpetuation of an institution that he demands in the life of the world. If he has a right to stay outside the Church, then every other good man has right to stay outside of the Church. The ultimate status of the Church under such conditions would be tragic indeed— there would be no Church. I keep ever in the heart of every one of these suggestions, the moving, warming spirit of a living, loving Christ attempting to win His brother back to the Father's home.

When the workers meet the answer, "I do not feel like it," I attempt to help them by giving them this statement: that feeling is not an infallible proof that the Son of Man is knocking at the heart's door; that there is great danger of emphasising feeling beyond its legitimate proportions. Feeling should not be placed first in this consideration. The question is not, "Do I feel like it?" It is rather, "Should I do it?" Feeling comes as an accompaniment to a good decision. We are somewhat to blame for this misplaced emphasis. I am perfectly frank to tell a person who is troubled thus that thousands have been misled at this point. Our fathers had so much to say about feeling that some of us were made to believe that it was the thing of most consequence. The only possible way for

Jesus to get into the heart of a man is through his brain. This may sound dogmatic, but it is not. It is true that a man who is wrong and sinful should have a change of heart, but he can never get a change of heart until he changes his mind. When a man does change his mind, then the Heavenly Father will be sure to change his heart.

It is at this point that a man's spiritual destiny is settled. If he chooses to remain stubborn and rebellious, all the spiritual forces on earth can not change his life. I talked for over an hour with a man one night in Tipton, Iowa. We went back and forth over this old battlefield where so many young people have died spiritual deaths because they tried to get the feeling of their fathers and mothers. When I finally succeeded in convincing him that his attitude was wrong, his significant statement was, " Then I have been taught wrong. It seems reasonable that if I accept Jesus, seek His pardon for lost time and sins committed, He will accept me ; but all of my life I have stayed outside of the Church and have refused to become a Christian because I was not able to have the experience that my parents used to talk about." This is the first thing that must be done ;—to persuade men and women to accept Jesus Christ at His word and the emotional element will have its place; but with this kind of an emphasis, the emotional suasion that comes to a man as he clasps the hand of Christ and in a perfectly natural and manly way swears his allegiance to his Heavenly Friend, will be used in substantial Christian service, instead of being dissipated in more or less selfish ecstasy.

As the evenings of the week pass, we deal with all of the questions that come up out of the work in the homes of the people. When this group has finished the week's work, they have become skilled in the art of meeting without argument or offense the questions that come as they continue in the blessed enterprise of evangelising their community.

IX

CONTINUOUS EVANGELISM

EVERY church should have a program of evangelism which produces results all of the time. Sporadic attempts are disappointing. Spasmodic evangelistic projects disorganise the regular work of the church and fail to lead to the most wholesome results. Normal Christians bear fruit regularly if they are organised to work systematically. If they are not directed in a definite enterprise, they flounder, and the God-given ambition to bring folks back to the Heavenly Father is drowned beneath other ambitions less spiritual.

Visitation Evangelism furnishes a continuous program for every church. The first "intensive" campaign demonstrates to the whole church that laymen can succeed in this work. It creates a passion for souls. The people who do the work are zealous to continue it; the people who observe their efforts are led to enroll as workers.

On the last night of the "intensive" campaign the visitors should be organised into a permanent committee on evangelism. The pastor should always be the chairman. I proceed by asking the workers, "What would you think of organising so that we may continue this work the year around?" There is always a unanimous vote. The people are eager to do it; they have been caught in the contagion of this experience.

Then I outline the work of the committee thus: There are two things this committee can do. They can continue at the call of the pastor to do this work. A few weeks after this "intensive," they should call upon the indifferent people of the church who have ceased to attend Divine worship. This is the most effective church attendance campaign that can be conducted, for these people have been actually fitted by their experience in the visitation campaign to make a winsome and persuasive appeal. I suggest to them when they go to these homes of church members who have lost out in the church, to appeal to them in this manner: to inform them that the church just recently has received into its membership fifty, one hundred and fifty, or two hundred, whatever the number may be; that it is one of the great triumphs, if not the greatest triumph, that their church has ever had; that it would be a spiritual disaster of far-reaching consequence if their church were to fail in properly training, nurturing, and directing these new Christian disciples; that, therefore, it is quite necessary that the people who are already members of the church should consecrate themselves to the task of establishing these new members in the life and heart of their fellowship. This is a far greater appeal than to go to an indifferent church member and say, " We should like to have you come to church—we think you should come to church." This type of invitation smacks too much of the argument of duty for duty's sake. It doesn't get a very big response. The first invitation here mentioned reveals the heart of Jesus to the man who has allowed other things to take the place of his Lord.

The Committee should be divided into three sub-committees:

1. Committee on Church Letters.
2. Committee on Christian Decision.
3. Committee on Infant Baptism.

This third committee, of course, would not be needed in a church which does not practise Infant Baptism.

These Committees are furnished with the information necessary for their work in this way: the Sunday school and every Society and Auxiliary of the church should have an Information Blank to be filled out by each person who enrolls. For example, suppose that a child enrolls in the Sabbath school and the information on his card reveals the fact that his father and mother are members of a church somewhere else. It will be the duty of the Committee on Church Letters, always co-operating with the pastor, to see that some team of persons gets to that home at once and secures their transfers. It is much easier to get people to transfer their membership during the first six months of their residence in a place than it is after they have been there six years, and many people have lost their religious habits within a much shorter time than that. Suppose again that this Information Card reveals the fact that there is someone in the home who has never made a Christian decision. It will then be the duty of the Committee on Christian Decisions to go to this home immediately and make an appeal for a Christian decision. Suppose, in the third place, that the Information Card handed in, we will say from the Men's Bible Class, shows the fact that there is an infant child in the home. It will be the duty of the Committee on Infant Baptism, co-operating with the pastor, to go to this home or send someone to invite these people to dedicate their child to God in Christian baptism. This will furnish one of the best opportunities to make an appeal to the child's father and mother, that they consecrate their lives to God and assist Him in training their child in religious habits and in Christian conduct. The pastor will probably have some method whereby he gets information concerning the visitors and transients who attend the public services of worship. This information would be classified by the Committee and used in the same way as the Information Card mentioned above.

Any church that will follow this method will be

in immediate and constant contact with a very large percentage of its constituency all of the time. There will be continuous accessions to the church. At Wesley Methodist Episcopal Church in New Bedford, Mass., we left an organisation of this kind, just as we leave them in all of the churches where we hold a campaign. The members continued their work; and while we had won one hundred and fifteen people during the five days of the campaign, at the end of the Conference year they had won and received into church membership a total of two hundred and twenty-seven, the largest number received by any church in the New England Southern Conference that year. In a little church of two hundred and two members in the city of Chicago, we urged the people to continue this work. While we were there we won one hundred and thirty-two new members. Nine weeks after the campaign, they had gained more than two hundred new people, and had more than doubled their membership in the short period of ten weeks. In St. Paul's Methodist Episcopal Church at Cedar Rapids, Iowa, they won more people during the two months following the campaign than they did in the immediate campaign.

This is the kind of evangelism that leaves the regular working force of the church far stronger at the close of the campaign than it is at the beginning. Any one who directs this method in any church is able to leave with this church a system that becomes an indispensable part of their program for the establishment of the commonwealth of Jesus upon earth.

III

THE DISCOVERIES OF VISITATION EVANGELISM

X

CONVERSION AND VISITATION EVANGELISM

JESUS gave us a splendid example when He talked with Andrew, Peter, Philip, Nathanael, Matthew, Nicodemus, and Mary Magdalene. The records show that Jesus was far more interested in the person's attitude toward Him and His Father than He was in any definition of conversion. These stories indicate to us that all a person needs to do in order to become a Christian is to follow Jesus.

What does it mean to be a follower of Jesus? To be a follower of Jesus means to be willing to live like Jesus, to love like Jesus, to work like Jesus, and, if necessary, to suffer for the welfare of your friends like Jesus. Often during the history of the Christian Church we have become so tangled up with certain sectarian trappings that we have lost sight of the most important consideration and experience. We have muttered religious formulas. Jesus has been obscured by partial statements of the truth about this or that matter. We have tried to force all kinds of temperament through the same kind of a religious experience at the time of con-

version. The time has come when we should take
Jesus at His own word and believe Him when He
says, "He that follows Me, let him take up his
cross," or "Whosoever will, may come," or "I am
come that ye might have life and that ye might have
it more abundantly"; therefore the type of conversion that we emphasise in visitation evangelism
is the type that Jesus emphasised.

All that we require is that the person, after thorough and careful description of what it means to
be a follower of Jesus, consent to be a disciple. We
ask each person if he is willing to receive Jesus
Christ as Saviour and to confess Him as his Lord
and Master; if he is willing to receive and profess
the Christian faith as taught in the New Testament
of our Lord Jesus Christ; if he will be loyal to the
Church and uphold it by his prayers, his presence,
his gifts, and his service. If he can answer these
questions in the affirmative then we have him sign
the following statement:

> I accept Jesus Christ as my personal
> Saviour, and purpose with His help to live
> a Christian life and do all I can to carry
> out His entire program. I desire to unite
> with the church of my choice and plan to
> present myself for membership one Sun-
> day removed from the date of this
> conversation.

Dr. Herbert Scott, Pastor of First Methodist
Episcopal Church, Des Moines, Iowa, said at the

Des Moines Annual Conference of the Methodist Episcopal Church, September 19, 1924, before a great gathering of ministers and laymen, " Do you ask me if the people are converted when this method is used? I will answer you as Dr. Charles L. Goodell answered the same question once: ' I do not know :—but they are showing the fruits of the Christian life.' This is really a pragmatic test. It is the only test that I care anything about."

XI

THE REACTION OF THE WORKERS

IF there were no other result from a Visitation
Evangelism campaign than the reaction upon
the workers, every church in the world would
be justified in undertaking such an enterprise.
Laymen grow spiritually in this work.

There are three discoveries that a layman makes
in this work. First, he discovers himself. There
are comparatively very few people who live their
own lives. Most people live as they do because of
sectarianism, partisanship, and custom. Only now
and then do we find a person who has courage
enough to discover what he has that is peculiar to
his own personality and then contribute that with
a beautiful self-abandon to some high and holy
end. This is true in all walks of life. It is true
in religion. The man who engages in visitation
evangelism goes out into the community with the
realisation that his success depends entirely upon
himself and his Christ. When he sits down to talk
with some neighbour he realises that the issue of
that conversation depends, to a large extent, upon
whatever persuasive abilities he may have to place
at the disposal of the Holy Spirit in that interview.

Straightway he is driven back upon his own resources. Very soon he discovers that he has persuasive abilities in this work that he never dreamed he possessed. He has always had an ambition to win somebody to the Christian life. His ambition has been realised. He comes back to church with a yearning for further conquests, a contagious anticipation of success, and a modest self-confidence which makes him very much like Jesus. Every campaign of this kind leaves in the church a number of laymen who have been transformed in the midst of their work.

In the second place, he discovers opportunity for service that he knew nothing about. As a matter of fact, the only way for a church to know its community is to know it through the home. The only way to know what people are aspiring to, what weights of discouragement and sorrow they have holding their spirits down, and the spontaneous response there is to a spiritual challenge everywhere —is to talk to them in the intimacy of their homes.

I arrived very early one Sunday morning in the city of St. Albans, Vermont. I took my bags to the Inn. I was very tired and nervous. It occurred to me that a little walk out in the fresh air of the morning would do me good. I went out, walked past a row of public buildings on one side of the Park, up Main Street, then up Congress Street, passed the parsonage, came back to the Inn, and sat down for a few moments. Then I got up

and went out and walked again. I saw a few
people going to the Roman Catholic Church, a few
others going out to play golf. I came back, sat
down and said to myself, " I have seen St. Albans."
I had seen it just as many others have—the outside
of the public buildings, the outside of the resi-
dences, the outside of the stores, and a few citizens.

I stayed there until Friday midnight. I saw a
dying man pleading with his pastor to be baptised
and received into the Church on his death-bed. I
saw his family going about with tears in their eyes
and emulating his example of Christian decision.
I met a young lady who told me that she had
always dreamed of serving God in some foreign
country. She was not even a member of the
Church. She made her Christian decision and we
made some suggestions that perhaps will ultimately
bring her to the goal of her ambition. I saw a boy
who had the light of that divine dream in his eye
which has led so many young men to become
Christian ministers. We assisted in starting some
communications with Boston University, which
probably resulted in his matriculation there. I saw
one hundred and three people become Christian disciples. I visited numerous homes where men who
had been out on strike a few months before had
scarcely enough money to provide food for the
family. I told them that some day the spirit of
Jesus would be so applied in industry that warfare
between employer and employee would cease, and

that their families would have a better chance. I tried to interpret Jesus' will toward employees. They responded in a wonderful manner. I might make the story longer, but you know it all now. When I went down and boarded the midnight train from Montreal to Boston and was quite by myself in the train, I said, " I have really seen St. Albans. I have seen the people where they dream and where they die; I have seen them where they live and where they love." I had seen the youth of the town fairly climb toward every altruistic challenge flung out before them in the name and in the spirit of Jesus. If the Church wants to keep her heart tender towards the needs of the world then the laity must visit in the homes.

The third discovery that a worker makes in this work is a new Christ. If we were to take the conception that we sometimes have of Jesus and stand it up along the side of our Saviour, we would cover our faces with shame. We have kept Jesus' quarters altogether too narrow. If a person is to have a robust, conquering Christ, he must see Him out in the community where the biggest things of the Kingdom of God must be done. When one sees Jesus conquer a man who has been selling himself for greed, and transform him into an obedient, sympathetic, Christian gentleman; then his conception of Jesus grows. When the worker sees Jesus draw a youth into the divine romance of an extraordinary spiritual goal; then his concep-

tion of Jesus assumes more appropriate proportions. When he sees Jesus redeem someone who
is badly lost, then his conception of Jesus is magnified and his confidence in Him is secure. These
are the priceless reactions that come in the mind
and the heart of any person who sincerely and
enthusiastically enters into the work of visitation
evangelism.

XII

ASSOCIATIONS FORMED DURING A VISITATION EVANGELISM CAMPAIGN

ONE of the serious problems before the Church is how to keep people who have already made their confession of faith interested and active. With the exception of a few fortunate churches, the pastor has had this task to do all alone. I am not overlooking the fact that the various organisations of the church render good service here, but I am pointing out the fact that about fifty per cent. of the people who are members of the church are not found in the services of worship. Quite naturally any pastor who anticipates an ingathering of any kind, seriously considers the danger of losing a large proportion of those who become members of the church.

There are several reasons why there has been such a terrible leakage in the past. One is that the people brought into the church were brought in almost entirely because of the work of a pastor or of an evangelist. If an evangelist had done the work, then, when he left the community, the person passed out of its life who above all others was closely joined to it by tender and beautiful associations established in the winning of its members to Christ. If the pastor had done the work, then he had scores of people dependent on him for the help that can come in its best form only from the one who was responsible for their conversion. Another reason for this loss of interest and discontinuance of church attendance, is the fact that the people who had had no particular part in their coming into the church often did not know them, and consequently, though they were ever so gracious, could not give them the warmth that is necessary for growth.

Another cause of this falling away from the church after the first step had been taken, is lack of training. Oftentimes no definition is given to a new member of his responsibility as a Christian. Of course, if most of the people in the church are failing to make the biggest religious urge practical in actual work in the community, then it is quite difficult for the minister, or anybody else, to instruct these people. The chill of the infidelity of those who belong is too much of a handicap. It doesn't make any difference how warm the weather is during the day, if a killing frost bites the flower at night. So it is in the church. The minister may radiate a boundless amount of spiritual warmth and energy, but he cannot keep the chill of indifference away from the new members.

Probably one of the most wonderful features of

this new method is that all three of these causes of
leakage in church membership and spiritual interest
are stopped, to a surprisingly large degree, by the
very nature of the work itself. There is all the
difference in the world in the permanency of evangelistic results in the work done by the pastor or
evangelist alone, and the work done by the pastor
and his laymen. The laymen, in the very process
of winning their friends and neighbours to Christ,
raise up associations between themselves and those
won that go on for ever and ever. The people who
have been won to this new relationship are now not
only held to the church by their loyalty to Christ,
but they are held to the church by a multitude of
heart-ties. The layman who sits down with his
neighbour and pleads with him, and then prays with
him, and sees the transformation that comes when
his neighbour accepts the new life, has formed a
relationship that assists the neighbour in feeling
absolutely at home in his friend's church, precludes
any possibility of indifference upon the part of the
neighbour toward the assimilation and establishment of his neighbour in the life of the church, and
becomes most convincing in teaching the new members. Now a minister does not define the Christian life by his teachings alone; but the members
of his church define the Christian life in the most
eloquent way possible—they live that definition.
This is the right kind of an environment in which
to train new converts. God help our churches to

realise more and more that they cannot import a revival: it must come up out of the hearts of the members. That is God's way of sending it down into a community.

After a campaign at Marshalltown, Iowa, the pastor made elaborate arrangements for the reception of two hundred and twenty-seven members into the Methodist Episcopal Church. There is a side entrance to his church which is used as the main entrance to the auditorium. He reserved the center section of pews the full length of the church for those who were to be received into membership that day. From this side door to the center section, he arranged the visitors in two lines. It was necessary for those who were to be seated in the center section to go between these two rows of workers to their seats. The pastor told me that he would remember that scene for ever. There a man would be going to his reserved seat and one of the workers would step forward and grip him by the hand and look into his face as he greeted him. He had won that man to his Christian decision. Here would come a woman. One of the ladies in the row would step forward, put her arm about the lady, and embrace her. She had won that woman to an acquaintanceship with Christ as her Saviour.

I am sure that it is all very plain and clear. Let us get rid of the heresy, quite widely accepted, that the minister is the only one who can explain what

it means to become a Christian. This is a harmful
and false impression.

When one of these visitation campaigns closes,
the church has an ideal situation so far as the
assimilation of these new members into the body
and spirit of the church is concerned. How easy
it is to say to the people who have been doing the
work, " I want you to become responsible for these
new members, assigning one or more of them to
each one of the workers. Get them into the various
organisations of the church; see that they come to
the weekly devotional meetings and get into the
various classes. In other words, you are to take
care of the establishment of these people in the
church and the Christian life."

XIII

WHAT THE CHURCH DISCOVERS

A church makes a number of significant discoveries in visitation evangelism. These discoveries tend to inspire the pastor, define the task of the church and bring in the Kingdom of God much more rapidly.

1. A church discovers a larger constituency than the members thought they had. We find that while the pastor of a church of a thousand members would estimate that he had six hundred in the community for whom his church was responsible outside of its membership, he is more likely to find that he has fifteen hundred or two thousand. There is always a tendency upon a part of the members of the church to underestimate their constituency. The only proper way to know actually how many people there are in any community for whom a church is responsible, is to take a religious census or survey of that community. This should be repeated every other year, or better, every year, in a community of any considerable size.

2. A church discovers many people who are ready to make a Christian decision. Some of these people are not suspected by anyone in the church

to be particularly interested in religion. The first
call that I made, after launching a campaign in
Chicago, was upon a family about four blocks from
a certain church. The mother and her two little
twin girls were at home. After I had visited with
the mother for a few moments, she commenced to
weep. I asked her what was troubling her and she
said, " Well, you know, Mr. Kernahan, when I was
a little girl I lived in this community and attended
this church. I sang in the choir for years. Then I
married and moved to the other side of the city.
We came back into this section seven years ago. I
have worked for six years to get my husband to
go to a Men's Bible Class. He has promised me to
go next Sunday."

I visited further with the lady, led her to make
her Christian decision, made arrangements for the
baptism of the little girls, and just as I was about
to leave, I said, " Mrs. R., I want to come and see
your husband tonight."

" No, please don't," she said. " He is very set
in his way, and if you come back, he will probably
refuse to go to the Bible Class next Sunday."

" Just trust me now," I replied. " If I do not
win your husband to an acquaintanceship with
Christ as his Saviour, I will not offend him."
After a good deal of persuasion she consented to
allow me to come back that evening. The little
girls had been listening carefully and they added
their sweet little invitations to me to come back.

I told Mrs. R. not to say anything about my coming.

The first thing after supper that evening I hurried over to the R. home. She had evidently forgotten her promise, for Mr. R. was sitting in the parlour all dressed up, ready to receive his caller. After visiting with him for a few moments and attracting the attention of the little girls, I began to make my appeal, with the little girls standing by my side.

"Dad," I said to him, "you don't want these little girls to be dedicated in Christian baptism while you remain apart from the church. There isn't anything in the world that you would not do to secure the moral and spiritual future of these little girls. You wouldn't refuse your wife the joy of having you by her side when she becomes a member of the church. Now, Mr. R., your wife is ready to make her confession of faith at the church altar and to have the little girls baptised. Are you not ready to be a Christian father, to walk in this new experience with your wife, to give your little girls your example?"

This man, whom his wife was even fearful to have me meet, took me by the hand, and giving me a hearty handshake said, "There isn't anything on earth that could keep me away from that church when my wife and girls go to the altar." Now, you see, he was all ready, and yet his wife had been talking to him for six years, trying to get him to go to a Bible Class. If we do less talking about church attendance to those who are not Christians, and more pleading for Christian decision, we would get further toward both goals.

3. A church discovers that her greatest power resides in the laity, that it is not necessary to bring in some professional evangelist; but that somebody who has been trained in inspiring the laity to do in a far more efficient manner what the professional evangelist used to do, will be of more lasting value. Dean Brown once said that there are three outstanding periods in Church history—the period of the martyr, the period of the monk, and the period of the Methodist, and they are everyone characterised by outstanding lay activity. Whenever a church makes progress, her interest must be carried forward in the minds and the hearts of the laity. It is not possible in one volume, or many, to describe the perfectly amazing results of the work of the laymen in the field of evangelism. There are multitudes of relationships and associations between the workers of the church and the people who are outside of the church, which may be capitalised in the work of evangelism. Laymen can talk in a much more intimate manner to their friends than to anyone else.

4. A church discovers that there is no bad aftermath when it engages in this method of evangelism. There has been nothing spectacular or sensational; there have been no bizarre headlines

in the newspapers. Those who are deep in sin have been approached in the spirit of Jesus. Invectives have not been hurled promiscuously from the pulpit. Conviction has not been preceded by anger. The motto has been: " Win a man, or leave him more friendly toward the Church than you found him." If you discover that you cannot win him gracefully, retreat, and leave him as open to an appeal as he was when you found him. The publicity in the campaign has been pretty much this type: Mrs. Grey has told Mrs. Brown across the lawn that the whole Martin family have made their decisions to come into the church a week from Sunday. This type of publicity has not built up antagonism and crystallised resistance. It has had a tendency to break down opposition and to mellow the whole field for evangelistic endeavour in the community. The visitors have become more enthusiastic as the days have passed. They come to the pastor during the last few days of work and say, " Do we need to discontinue this work Friday night? Can we not continue it longer? We are tired, but when we get a little bit rested, we would like to go on."

And this interest becomes cumulative. Perhaps two hundred have been won in a quiet, sincere, enthusiastic, loving way. These two hundred have a multitude of relationships. They become interested in their relatives and friends and are willing to go with the workers to visit them, and to use their influence to persuade them to become Christians. The weeks following a campaign of this sort are filled with spiritual romance. New families are always being discovered, further Christian decisions secured, until it seems that the field becomes more fertile for cultivation and production than it was before the campaign was launched. This is the ideal situation that the Church has always dreamed about, but was never able to realise before this method of evangelism was discovered.

5. A church finds that she has too big a task to perform to spend any time in narrow sectarianism. As the visitors go to work day after day, they find that their appeal has an appealing sincerity when they tell the folks upon whom they call that they have not come to ask them to be Methodist, or Episcopal, or Lutheran, or Congregationalist, or Presbyterian, or Baptist; but that they have come to invite them to become Christians and join the church they prefer. The denomination is quite immaterial. It doesn't make any particular difference what church a person belongs to, but it makes all the difference in the world whether a person accepts Jesus Christ as his leader, his Saviour, and his companion, and then becomes an efficient worker in some branch of Christ's Church. Every campaign that I have directed in two years of work has won people to churches that were not participating in the campaign and sent them to those churches to confess their faith in Christ and become active

members of that church. In a city-wide Methodist campaign in the city of Des Moines, Iowa, we sent more than one hundred people who had accepted Jesus Christ as their personal Saviour, to other churches. This has the most wholesome effect upon all of the churches, bringing them to a realisation that the task of winning a city for God is a common responsibility and that a man who accepts Christ, is a gain to every church. I have reached the point in my own thinking upon this matter where I frankly say, that I do not believe that any denomination should launch a campaign of this nature in a community, without first inviting the co-operation of every church in that community.

6. A church discovers that we have come to a period in Christian history when people are not at all interested in dogmatism. One of the tragedies of the Christian Church occurred when the leaders got all confused in a discussion of speculative questions during the first century of Church history. They commenced to fight back and forth and tried to tell all of the truth as they saw it in some particular statement. They became dogmatic, and while they were fighting about the proper way to wall Christian truths up in language, fearing that truth cannot take care of itself, they lost the whole continent of Africa. Then more recently various groups formed sects who were more interested in their creeds than they were in the people who were to accept them; and the whole world was over-

whelmed by religious shibboleths. We will have none of that today. The thing that people are most interested in now is, what does Christianity do for life? What virtue is there in following Jesus Christ as our standard-bearer? People are not particularly interested in what somebody said about Jesus five hundred years ago. They are interested in what Jesus has to say to them today.

Now, in this method, we do not go out to ask people if they will accept the teachings of the Scripture as interpreted by the doctrine of some church. We go out to ask them if they will accept Jesus Christ as their Saviour. We do not ask them to have our experience. We ask them to look upon Jesus and have their own experience. As a matter of fact, any other demand would be unfair, and would lead to the worst kind of hypocrisy. We go out to talk about the personality and the Saviourhood of Jesus. This kind of an approach immediately wins the respect of the thoughtful people in the community.

These are the discoveries that a church makes when sincerely, with all her heart, she arises from her pews and goes out into the community to apply the spiritual power which has been generated in her services of worship and teaching, to the task of winning men and women back to the Heavenly Father.

IV

GOD'S GREATEST HUMAN RESOURCE

XIV

PERSONALITY—GOD'S GREATEST RESOURCE IN CARRYING THE INVITATION

BISHOP CHARLES E. LOCKE was right when he said, a person does not need to search long in God's wonderful world before he comes to the conclusion that when God wanted to make His greatest creation He did not make a towering mountain, a tumbling sea, a sparkling jewel, a transcendent poem, a triumphant army—He made man; and the astonishing thing about this fact is that He made many of the tallest souls out of the humblest material. The greatest thing about man is his personality. The greatest resource that God has in this world is personality. Man has capitalised it in the commercial field with outstanding results. Teachers find it their biggest asset. Preachers succeed or fail just in proportion to the personality they possess, provided they are absolutely given up to their task.

It is astonishing how susceptible the people in any community are to the Christian appeal when it is delivered by an earnest, sincere neighbour. The results in this sort of work are convincing and emphatic. Suppose that out of the more than four million members in the Methodist Episcopal Church, one hundred thousand are enlisted to do this work. In one week they would win one million four hundred thousand to Christian discipleship. This is not a dream. If, in winning ten thousand people, the workers of all ages and degrees of ability averaged fourteen won per team each week of work, it is logical to conclude that an average of fourteen won per team is a correct estimate of future success.

We do not need more preaching nearly so much as we need people who will apply the spirituality generated in our services of worship to the task of persuading friends to accept Jesus and His program of living. Our public services of worship should be for the inspiration, education, and culture of our people. Our evangelism should be done just as Jesus did it—by personal contact and interview.

XV

SOME SUGGESTIONS IN TECHNIQUE

I AM afraid that spiritual laziness accounts for more tragedies in any community than any brand of depravity. Jesus' love for the world has been such a constant fountain of inspiration that some have been perfectly willing to use the "overflow" of His love in promoting small plans easily executed in the work of evangelism. We have failed to realise that if spiritual enterprises are to keep step with the advance made in other fields of thought and work in the world, it will be necessary to give proportionate attention to methods and organisation.

I have no sympathy with the church cynic who criticises programs and methods. A man who organises his spiritual work will do many times more the amount of good than the one who does not. Thousands and thousands of dollars are spent by every big concern on earth to train men of good personality to become salesmen. After they have once been trained, the tenure of the work with that concern depends entirely upon how much they sell. I have sometimes thought that it might be a good plan to place the same measure upon the work of a pastor. You may say, " Oh, no, there are so many other things that pastors do that you could not measure their success by the number of conversions." My answer is that it does not make any difference how many other things a minister does. If he does not succeed in persuading some of those who are not now Christians to become disciples of Jesus, he has failed. It would be of inestimable value to the Christian churches if they were to give special attention to the study of the technique of presenting the Christian appeal face to face with those who are not now Christians.

I once heard Dr. George Elliott, Editor of *The Methodist Review,* say that " one of the best proofs of the Divinity of the Church is the fact that there have been the least brains and money invested in it of any great institution on earth, and yet, here it is alive and doing business." He indicates here that success and progress have been made in the Christian Church in spite of her short-sighted, clumsy, bungling, unwise, inapt presentation of Jesus.

What any ordinary group of workers can do after receiving a few simple instructions in the technique of this wonderful enterprise is simply overwhelming. Here is an instance: The day after I had launched a simultaneous campaign in Toledo and Tama, Iowa, a man whom the pastor, Dr. Dewitt Clinton, had enlisted as a visitor, whose ability in this work was absolutely unknown either to himself or anybody else, came and asked for the card of a certain man. The pastor scarcely knew whether to give it to him. Pastors had failed for over thirty years to win this particular man to a public confession of his faith in Jesus Christ. He had been attending the church for years and was one of the most prosperous men in the community. Finally the pastor, rather reluctantly, gave this worker the card. He went to the man's home and visited with him about their mutual friend, Jesus. The result was that our friend then and there made his decision publicly to confess his faith in Christ and his loyalty to His Church.

The day after we launched the campaign in Omaha, Nebraska, a team called upon a man whose office was situated in the second or third best office building in the city of Omaha. After they had visited a few minutes, they discovered the following facts: The man's father was a Cumberland Presbyterian and had been a Sunday school superintendent for many years; his wife had been an active member of the Methodist Episcopal Church ever since he first met her; he had a boy eighteen years of age, who had gone away to school; he had lived in the city of Omaha nineteen years, and had gone to church three times during that period. You see, the workers had announced the purpose of their call, and then by direct and courteous questioning, they had gathered together this exceedingly valuable data.

One of the men acted as spokesman for the team

from that point on. He said to the man, "Do you mean to tell me that in all the lifetime of your boy, whom you say is eighteen years of age, you have gone to church but three times? Do you mean to say a little baby came into your home and that you allowed him to grow day after day without giving any attention whatsoever to your own religious vitality? Don't you know that the only God that a baby sees is the Heavenly Father that he discovers in the eyes of his mother and father? Can it be true that a little laddie used to trip along by your side and that you never led his little feet to the church and to the church school? Don't you see that you have surrendered the most glorious privilege that God ever gives a man? You could have built into the religious background of your boy's life a texture that would stand the strain of centuries. You could have given him an example of loyalty to the church and interest in spiritual nurture that would have become his most precious possession. Now your boy is gone. He probably never will be back again to stay permanently."

The man being interviewed first showed keen interest, then tremendous earnestness, finally a broken heart. Now, this man was important enough in the life of the city of Omaha to have his photograph carried upon the front page of the Omaha *Bee* in a series of articles entitled "Men That Are Making Omaha." What had happened to him all at once so far as his religious interest was concerned? Two men who had been told that to enter in upon the work of visitation evangelism, a man should apply the same spiritual and psychological principles to the presentation of a Christian religion as he does in salesmanship in the work of his everyday life.

They were having an adventure in the field of Christian conquest, by applying the same brain and the same earnestness in the work of Christ as they used in their everyday secular life. The wonderful thing about this is, that men who are successful in meeting the public in their everyday contacts, are much more successful when they commence to talk about Jesus. There is a fragrance in His personality, a beauty in His enterprise, and a romance about His conquest that fill a man's lips with eloquence, his heart with a spontaneity of expression, and his hands with an artistry in spiritual activities which cannot be equaled in any other work on earth.

XVI

OBSERVATIONS WHILE WINNING TEN THOUSAND PEOPLE TO CHRISTIAN DISCIPLESHIP

THE observations which have accumulated during the last few months of my work are of sufficient amount and cover an extensive enough field to furnish the basis for certain true conclusions. There are quite a large number of conclusions coming out of this work which are of sufficient importance to occupy space here.

1. There are no peculiar places. This method will work anywhere on earth. I have at hand a letter written by J. Harlow Graham, pastor of Trinity Methodist Episcopal Church, Norwich, Connecticut. He has gone through three visitation evangelism campaigns with me. One of them was conducted out in the country where there was no village whatsoever,—just a church. This was a decadent community in New England. It would not rank in its life or ability with most of the decadent communities in New England. Most of the people would say that there were scarcely any English-speaking inhabitants left—that practically all of the old farms had been taken over by Jewish

and Polish people. It was quite interesting to just keep count of those who told that there were no English-speaking people left, and then total that number. We found, for instance, twenty-one boys and girls who were born in English-speaking homes in less than one mile.

The second campaign was held in a downtown city church. The constituency was both industrial and business people. The third campaign was a city-wide project. In his letter, Rev. Mr. Graham says that six months afterward the results of the campaign were exactly the same. In other words, the proportion of people won to a Christian decision and membership per team was the same; that the permanency of the loyalty of those who were won was the same. We find that ninety-six per cent. of the people who are won to Christian decision by this method of visitation evangelism are in the churches giving attention to the religious life and bearing the fruits of a Christian citizen six months after the campaign. Here we have three distinct groups of people represented in three campaigns mentioned in this letter, and yet our results are identical. This has been my experience during the winning of ten thousand people. We have found that while communities differ in many respects, they do not differ in their response to an invitation given in love to accept and serve Jesus Christ.

2. Any sincere worker can do this work. He

does not need to be able to quote Scripture. He does not need to have an extensive religious background of training and experience. He does not need to be educated in every instance. It is not necessary that he be accustomed to the work of meeting people in his everyday work. If you will recall the folks whom Jesus won, you will find several very distinct types of people. There was Peter, a man with natural eloquence; there was Mary Magdalene, a woman with a broken life; there was Zacchæus, a man hated because he was connected with the enemy government.

3. If the minister makes an appeal to his people individually, he will get a larger number to do this work than he ever dreamed would consent to do it. He will get people to do this work who have not been in the limelight of the church's life. Some who will be the most successful will be those whom he least expected to succeed.

4. The pastor finds that the people who do the work clarify their own Christian faith. They are attempting to put into their own language a definition of their Christian faith. They become definite, direct, and attractively confident. The mayor of St. Albans, Vermont, said with a good deal of feeling, " Why, Mr. Kernahan, I could not do this; this is not in my line." I encouraged him, pleaded with him to try it, hurried him out of the church to his task, and when he came in with his report, you would have thought that he had met Jesus down

the street in actual bodily form. "You never could have convinced me that it was possible," he said, "but now I know. We won so-and-so to Christ tonight."

In Chicago a certain young lady promised to do this work because she did not want to disappoint her pastor. She was naturally very reticent. We sent her out with another young lady who was a bit more aggressive in temperament. I went in the other direction from that taken by this team of young ladies. About an hour and a half later I heard someone call about a half a block away, "Oh, Mr. Kernahan!" I was surprised to hear anyone calling my name on the street, for I had been in the community but a few hours. I was doubly surprised to find that it was this reticent young lady. I do not know whether girls ever throw their hats in the air, but I would not have been surprised to have seen this girl throw her hat in the air as she called with the music of heaven in her voice, "Oh, Mr. Kernahan, we have won four!"

Oftentimes the person who is most sure that he cannot do this work becomes the most remarkable success in it because the timidity which causes him to hesitate to undertake it, gives him a beauty about his appeal which the over-confident cannot possess. This young lady in Chicago said afterward, "I did not know how I was going to be able to tell anybody else how to be a Christian. I have discovered that all I need to do is to talk about my friend and

Saviour, Jesus, just as I would about any other person, with the added realisation that He can be a greater help and blessing to the person I am talking to than anyone else on earth."

5. The worker oftentimes can win people to a Christian decision whom the pastor cannot win. At the First Methodist Episcopal Church of Sioux City, Iowa, the pastor made this remark at the conclusion of a campaign: " One of the most remarkable features about this work is the fact that I have tried to win fully sixty per cent. of these people who have been won by my workers, and I failed." He was simply expressing what every pastor with whom I have worked has discovered.

6. Many men and women can be won who have passed through scores of revival meetings without making their decisions. In the city of Des Moines, Iowa, we won a man past ninety years of age who had been active in the business life of the city. " I have always believed in Christ," he said. " I think that this world would be hopeless without Him. I wondered if there was not some way whereby I could talk this thing through and make my decision in my home where I make most of my decisions. You may tell the pastor that I will be at church a week from Sunday morning to make my confession of faith. I am sorry that someone did not come to me in this fashion seventy years ago or more. My decision then would have been exactly the same as it is now." His type is legion.

7. Another observation is that there are thousands and thousands of people who have been touched by the teaching and preaching ministry of the church, who have never been asked to make a definite Christian decision to become members of the church. In one of the Eastern cities, I called one afternoon upon the leading citizen in the community. My team-mate was a judge of distinction and ability. This man had been in politics for over forty years. He had always had a more or less definite relationship with one of the churches. We finally persuaded him to accept Jesus Christ as his Saviour and to become an active Christian worker in the community. He told us that while he had been in politics for forty years and had been approached by the men of the community upon almost every matter of civic interest and social welfare, he had never been asked in his life to make a decision for Christ, confess his faith, and join the Church.

8. Perhaps one of the most interesting observations that we have made in this work is that there are very few people outside of the Church who realise that, if they believe in Jesus Christ as the Saviour of the world, the confession of that faith and relationship in the church is an inevitable responsibility. Our message in the past has had so much to do with the individual emphasis that there are very few who realise at all that there is such a thing as social responsibility. They have been led to believe by long years of preaching that whether

they chose to be active members in the Christian Church was entirely an optional matter; while as a matter of fact, if we study the progress of the human race, we know that anyone who starts out with the belief that Jesus Christ is the Saviour of the world, must espouse His cause and invest his personality in the Christian Church. History is a series of reforms written in the blood of those who have given themselves to Christ's Church. If I accept Christ as the Saviour of the world, then to be consistent I must assist Him to become the Saviour of my community.

I visited a judge in a Middle Western city one day, and after a few moments of pleasant conversation about the religious background of his boyhood, he said, " I do not know what I would give for the blessings that have been given me because of the religious life of my parents."

" Then," I said to him, " of course, you will pass those same blessings on to posterity by giving your life to the promotion of the religious interests of the community."

" Oh, I believe in the Christian life," he replied, " and we want the churches, but whether I become a member of the church or not, is quite immaterial."

" Judge," I answered, " you would punish a man for that kind of an argument in your court procedure. You expect every man who is brought before you to return just compensation for every service rendered him. Now, we cannot make that analogy go down on all fours, but this one thing is the same in each instance. You likewise will expect to compensate the church and Christian environment for what they have given you. If the matter of *your* church membership is immaterial, then the membership of *every other* person is immaterial; and if we all considered church membership immaterial, there would be no Church. The only thing in this wide world that will perpetuate a Christian Church is the gift of sincere lives."

"I never thought of it from that standpoint before," said the judge. "I believe you are correct. I am determined to serve Jesus Christ in the way you suggest. I will be present a week from Sunday morning to make my confession of faith and be received into the church."

9. I have observed that we have raised a partition between our expressions of religious devotion and our civic life. We have actually talked so much about separation of State and Church that we have not only accomplished in our minds the organic separation which is good, but the spiritual separation which is bad. I have found a large number of men who were responsible for the political program of the civic life of the community who say that good people are quite vociferous in demanding certain types of government and reform, but fail to function in a practical manner when it comes to supporting any program of this nature which they might desire to put over. We won the mayors of

four different cities in four successive campaigns. They all said that now they had taken their stand for Christ in the Church, they were going to use their influence in arousing the Church to the necescity of getting behind and staying behind every good man who entered politics.

These conclusions have been drawn after careful tabulations of innumerable interviews with men and women about Christian decision and Christian citizenship.

V

THE EVANGELISM OF THE CHANGE-LESS CHRIST

XVII

THE CHANGELESS CHRIST AND EVANGELISM

CHANGE is written in large letters across the face of the universe. We find it where we least expect to find it. I am told by scientists that if you take a bar of steel and a bar of brass and place them very close together and leave them for a considerable length of time, and then analyse them, you will find molecules of the steel bar in the brass, and molecules of the brass bar in the steel. Consequently, the only conclusion you can come to is that these two hard metals are in constant change and motion. We speak of the everlasting mountains, yet they are being constantly smoothed upon the top by the play of the elements and tunneled beneath by the genius of man's hand. Change is everywhere. I have seen it ingrained upon the peaks of the mountains, and crocheted upon the profiles of the hills by great railroad trunk lines.

When I was a boy, I had the privilege of hearing one of those unusual speakers who was able to take all of the experiences of the people who sat before him and make them preach marvelous sermons.

Later, he was elected a Bishop in the Methodist Episcopal Church and was retired at their General Conference held in Springfield, Massachusetts, in May, 1924. I am speaking of William A. Quayle. His address that day made a lasting impression upon me. His language was so homely and his delivery so unique that one of the paragraphs of that address still stays in my memory. It was not a definition of change but a description of change given in his poetic manner. Here it is: " You remember a schoolhouse where the world was at its widest; the fishing stream; the swimming pool; the scramble up the bank with bruised feet; the spring at which you used to recline and drink and drink and drink and drink and yet you were never satisfied; the spankings wherewith your relatives regaled you that you never got one too many; the chores; the Saturdays; the first indications of Spring; the stopping amid fields to see the sullen splendour of a cloud burned low like a great ship in conflagration." These things he said were the commonplace things of the past. The humdrums and stupidities of life. They were the hardy makers of our souls, but they were gone, never to return.

Scientific theories change. I remember that, when at college, we had a certain scientific theory which was at the basis of our investigation in a certain department of chemistry. We supposed that that theory was as changeless as the laws of the Medes and the Persians. We even referred to it as a law. I had not been graduated from college long, however, when I was informed that that theory had proven false and that all future experiments in that department of chemistry would be based upon a new theory.

Forms of government change. There has been a constant succession in changes of government from the old Patriarchal down to the Presidential— the best form of government God ever smiled upon. I cannot mention governments any more without digressing long enough to say that I am fearful that there are many people in the United States of America who have no idea of the cost of this government. It has evolved through agony and bloodshed which no tongue or pen will ever be able to describe adequately, but it has come to us through a series of changes.

We change ourselves. Some of the things we used to love, we hate; and some of the things we used to hate, we love. Our old homesteads change. A few years ago I was discharged from the Army at Camp Dix, New Jersey. I started off across the long miles to my native home in the Middle West. I had no more than taken my seat in the Pullman car and the locomotive had started, when the wheels commenced to sing songs of other days. Now, a young person may not understand this, but anyone who is older, who has sat a long distance from some fond destination and has allowed the memories of

yesterday to come trooping back through his mind,
has observed that any rhythm will take upon itself
the clothing of words, and straightway come songs
of yesterday. As I sat in the car through the first
day and attempted to sleep during the first night,
the old car wheels went on singing their songs. I
could again see my boyhood home out there in the
country eight miles from Oelwein, Iowa. I could
see the little dining room where mother would
spend the long winter evenings, and there were my
brothers and sisters, George, Julius, Mae, and Belle.
I heard the old stories again that Mother used to
tell, stories about the early hardships of the Middle
West; and about a trip across from South Dakota
to Iowa in a prairie schooner. There in my mind's
vision was the old home, just as it used to be. Of
course I knew that it had changed, but I was in one
of the moods in which a man is easily deceived if
he be not careful to check up upon the natural readjustments which have come to him. When I arrived in Iowa I found that old home all gone.
One sister had been called long ago to a home that
was far superior to anything we could provide for
her, and we soon ceased to complain. My brother
had been burned to death during the war. Another
sister was living in a home upon the Pacific Coast,
another brother in a new home in the Middle West,
Mother in another home, and I on the Atlantic
Coast. The old home was absolutely gone—never
to return.

I believe that I understand human nature somewhat, and I am surely telling the truth, when I say that in the midst of this change, transition and chaos, the deepest instinct of the human soul is to reach up and get hold of something that does not change, preferably a personality. There has been but one system of thought, philosophy, or religion that has ever presented a person who has been eternally changeless in the qualities that make him like God. There has been but one Person who, irrefutably, has declared Himself, through the centuries, to be changeless in the virtues that make Him stand out like a giant mountain in a mountain range. I am speaking of Jesus.

If I were to do the next logical thing in the pursuance of this thought, I would attempt to prove that Jesus is changeless. I am not going to do the logical thing. I ask you to consider a more fundamental question. The question is not as to the changelessness of Jesus, but concerning Jesus Himself. If the reader happens to have been trained in the same kind of school as I was, please be patient. If you feel that we have no right to enter upon this ground, I beseech you to consider the thousands and thousands of young men and young women in our high schools and colleges who are more interested in this question than in any other consideration that has to do with religion. Down there in those years of natural doubt and necessary readjustments, they are looking toward us and asking " Who is Jesus and what is Jesus?" What do we usually do when one from this group, or perchance someone from an older group, asks this question? We usually do nothing, and when we realise that there are hundreds who are thinking it but do not ask it, then the seriousness of this situation dawns upon us. I say, we usually do not do anything. It has been my experience that only one person in fifty ever talks about Jesus in his regular everyday life in a contagious manner. These people are trying to discover by our conversation whether we actually think that Jesus is real. We remain silent.

There is at least one reason for this silence. Here it is: We look into the face of Jesus and we see a beauty there that cannot be comprehended within a sentence, a paragraph, or a book; and we say, "Who can define Jesus in absolute terms?" We look into His personality, and we see a power there that has transformed the thought of the ages, renovated the social life of millions of people, changed customs and let in the sunlight of a wholesome philosophy of life which has already started to set up the Kingdom of God on earth. We say it is impossible to define Jesus in absolute terms. Here is the fallacy. Just because we discover that we cannot define Jesus in absolute terms, we should not cease to talk about Him. As a matter of fact, we cannot define anything that has life in it in absolute terms. Religious creeds are very helpful, but they are never absolutely true. That is the wonder about Jesus. That is the romance in Christianity; for Christianity is life, not creed. We do not insist upon defining many things in terse and explicit sentences which we talk about in a persuasive and contagious way.

Think, for instance, of four of our indispensable possessions. What is beauty? I was at one time pastor of First Methodist Episcopal Church, Northampton, Massachusetts. There is a wonderful old street in that city called Elm Street. It is skirted on either side by giant trees. They are so large and so old that it is necessary to put bands of steel around some of them to keep the limbs from breaking down. On my way to the church every Sunday morning, I walked beneath the spreading limbs of these old trees. I was always in a tender mood to catch any suggestion that might make me a better preacher that morning, and many times, in fact I think always, I would look out between these limbs over the steeple of my church located on the corner of Smith College Campus, and see in the distance a little mountain. They called it Mount Tom. I would say to myself, " Isn't the mountain majestic this morning, holding its head up high in the heavens, worshipping God? Isn't the mountain beautiful? "

Later, I was pastor of a church in Boston, Massachusetts. Just to the right of the pulpit stood the erect, superb figure of Jesus. Now I knew that that picture worked into a stained glass window was the result of the best dreams of an artist. I do not know just how much that picture looked like Jesus when He was upon earth. I think, however, that the artist must have seen Jesus some sunlit morning, for there was a beauty upon that face that was matchless.

One day I was out in the middle of the ocean, upon the largest passenger ship owned by France. I was sitting far out at the stern and I saw a storm come staggering across the sea. One of the biggest dreams that I had as a boy and a young man, was to see a storm at sea. This may seem strange, for I was born and had lived nearly all my life in the Middle West. I was so green about the ocean that I felt like doing what a friend of mine said he felt like doing when he first saw the ocean. I wanted to get down on my knees and taste the water to see whether it had any salt in it. But here I was face to face with one of the big experiences that I had always yearned after. I almost tied myself aboard and stretched out over the stern to see the storm that came wading on with giant strides towards us. It was beautiful. The heavens put on a mourning that I did not know even the fingers of God could weave and hang across the early day. The angry ocean churned up a thousand colours until, as you looked upon the crest of every wave, it seemed as though you were looking into a fairy park studded with myriads of jewels.

I walked back into the middle of the ship and

stood with thousands of men about me. They were crossing the sea to enter into another storm. They were dreaming about it. It was already raging in their hearts. The marks of it were upon their faces. They were experiencing already the pain, hate, and mental anguish of the war. "This is beautiful," I said, "the sky, the wind, the sea, the brain, and the heart of men all in a strain and struggle."

Now, I have been talking about beauty. I think that I have been talking about it contagiously. I do not believe that anyone would doubt that I believe there is such a thing as beauty. But what is it? Somebody says it is a harmonious relationship of parts. That's no definition. I have seen some girls who could arrange powder and hair very harmoniously, but there was no beauty there. What is poetry? Somebody says it is the voice of the soul, but that's no definition. We have not yet been able to define the soul. What is the home? Somebody answers, "Why, the home is four walls, the ceiling, the floor, and a man and woman who have been joined in the holy bonds of matrimony." That's not a definition. You present to me a man and woman who love each other and have been joined together in the holy bonds of matrimony, and you have a home without a house. Was it not Mark Hopkins who said, "What is a college? A log with a professor at one end of it and a student at the other. That's a college." What is genius?

Abraham Lincoln was a genius, but there have been scores of books written about Abraham Lincoln, and the one thing that they cannot explain is his genius.

Do we cease to talk about these indispensable possessions of the human race? Do we refuse to accept their contributions to our lives? How about beauty? When I am in the midst of beauty, I drink it in; and that same beauty courses down through my personality and becomes a ministry to the folks. How about poetry? Just because I cannot tell you in explicit terms what poetry is, do I refuse to receive what it has to enrich my life? Is this poetry?

> " The American finds not in this wide world a
>   pleasure so sweet
> As to sit at the window and tilt up his feet,
> And puff away at his Cuba whose flavour
>   just suits,
> And gaze at the world 'twixt the toes of his
>   boots."

How about this?

> " He gathers our prayers as He stands,
> And they change into garlands in His hands,
>   Into flowers of purple and red;
> And beneath the wide arch of the portal,
> Through the streets of the city immortal,
>   Is wafted the fragrance they shed."

What is the difference between these two selections? One is poetry, the other is not. Now, just because I cannot define poetry in absolute terms, shall I deny to the mind of some unusual person the privilege of reaching up into the skies and gathering up the screech of the shells that went on their deathward march a few years ago, the cries of the men who burned to death up there; of reaching down into the bowels of the sea and gathering up the murmurs of the babies who drowned down there; of reaching out over the blood-soaked battlefields and gathering up the prayers and the profanities of the boys who fought over there; and mixing them all together in the magic of his personality, to pour out an epic into the minds and the hearts of the people? No, we will accept his songs, and some day, in the midst of depression, we will find that the songs we cannot define have become the means of our escape.

Now, how about the home! Just because I cannot tell you what the home really is, shall I deny the arms of a woman the privilege of holding her offspring and breathing into his face the dreams of a hundred mornings? No, rather we shall say, "Go on. Make your contribution to the needs of this day, furnish God the first generation that ever anywhere nearly approximated Jesus' ideal of world citizenship."

What shall we do about genius? We cannot define it, and yet this is the day of genius. One morning I was leaving a hotel to go to a pulpit where I was to preach. Just as I passed through the lobby, I heard a beautiful song somewhere. The clerk said, " Sit down a moment." I did, and for the next ten minutes I enjoyed a religious service. I said, " Where is this service being held?" The clerk informed me that it was Omaha, Nebraska. I heard the people singing that beautiful old hymn, " Who Could It Be But Jesus?" I heard the preacher pray, and as he became the mouthpiece of his congregation and prayed for the wide world that morning, I felt that genius was acquainting us, better than we had ever before realised, with our Heavenly Father.

It is surely fair to suggest that we should take exactly the same attitude toward Jesus. Of course we cannot define Him. Words are too forced and rigid. Jesus cannot be tied down to this earth in the cold shackles of a definition, but we can talk about Him with a greater certainty and contagion than we can about beauty, poetry, home, or genius —and the consequences are more needful.

I am not saying that we cannot have a practical definition of Jesus. May I suggest it in this way? Many of the so-called laws of nature were not discovered until some men were willing to pay the price of incarnating them in their own being. Men died for centuries and passed by herbs that had medicinal properties in them that would have cured their diseases, until some doctors gave the health-giving properties contained in these herbs to the world. Men died upon ships and were buried in the sea, and all that was necessary for them to do was to speak through the proper kind of an instrument thousands of miles away to receive the aid which would have saved their lives. Then Edison commenced to think, Marconi thought a bit further, and they gave to the world wireless telegraphy. A man named Newton observed an apple fall down and he said, " If the apple falls down instead of up, there must be some reason." He commenced to co-operate with God in his willingness to serve, and eventually discovered a certain law, and he gave it to the world as a law of gravitation. Just as Newton, Edison, Marconi, and others, are the incarnation of natural laws; so Jesus is the incarnation of the love, of the will, and the purpose of God. This makes our work simple. As we go out to talk about religion, we do not need to talk in abstractions or platitudes. We are to talk about Jesus. He personifies the teachings of our Heavenly Father. All we need to have is capacity for friendship and acquaintanceship with Jesus to be assured of success. Jesus dramatises in the most eloquent way all of the teachings of God to us.

We have been thinking about Jesus, about the changeless Jesus. Let us talk about the three ways in which Jesus does not change.

1. He does not change in His teachings. We change in our interpretations of His teachings, but when we fathom what He really taught in reference

to any particular relationship of life or about life itself, we can be sure that these teachings will never change. I am glad that we do change in our interpretations of His teachings. We are more nearly approximating the truth as the years go by.

I once boarded a train in a small city about three hundred miles from Chicago. After we had traveled a few miles, I found that my seat companion was also a preacher. He was a minister of a denomination I am not acquainted with in any intimate way. I said to him, "This is a great privilege for me. I do not suppose in my whole life that I have had an opportunity to visit with a man of your denomination as long as I shall today, and if you do not mind, I would like to ask you one question about your Church. Do you still teach that if a baby dies who has not been baptised, he is lost?"

He seemed rather reticent in answering.

Then I asked him again, "Does your Church still teach that if a baby dies without being baptised, he is lost?"

"We have no right to teach that he is saved," he said.

"Brother," I replied, "I am sure that I have the right to look into the face of any broken-hearted mother and tell her that when death breaks the little chubby arms away from her bosom, the baby spirit goes directly to the bosom of the Father, whether he has been baptised or not. That is the only environment for a baby-spirit when he leaves the arms of his mother."

Now, the purpose of the story is this: There are many still living who remember when there were at least a half-dozen denominations or small branches of denominations that were teaching that babies who die without baptism are lost. I thank God that we do change in our interpretations of Jesus' teachings. I could take you to a score of cemeteries today where little headstones stick themselves up outside of the cemetery walls as monuments to this superstition. Thank God we are moving away from that, but Jesus remains ever the same in all of His teachings. When we change our teachings, we are simply getting nearer to Jesus.

If you were converted, my reader, after you became adult, the first ambition that you had when you became acquainted with Jesus as your Saviour, was to go home or out in the community and win somebody else to Christ. He taught you in that first wonderful experience that it was possible for you to take enough of His beauty into your face, His winsomeness into your voice, and His passionate love into your heart to go out and win scores to a Christian discipleship. If He is not teaching you that today, you have lost your contact with your teacher. He will teach His loyal followers that, as long as there is one man upon earth who has not become His friend. That is a sentimental teaching but absolutely fundamental to the redemption of the world. Jesus has put this at the very basis of any evangelistic program. It was prerequisite to His own success. It is likewise absolutely indispensable if the modern church is to make the advance that looks very possible.

2. Jesus does not change in His attitude toward lost people. Do you remember what it was? They brought before Him a woman that was taken in sin. Jesus stooped His face in modesty, the modesty of a Saviour. "If anyone of you men who brought this woman here is without sin," He said, "you cast the first stone"; and, while He waited, He wrote some words in the sand, the only words we have any record of His writing. When He lifted His face He looked deep down into the heart of the woman and said, "What, is there no man here to condemn you?"—for the men had all slipped away.

"No, Lord," she answered, "there is no one here to condemn me."

"Neither do I condemn you," Jesus said. "Go, and sin no more."

Christ's attitude was that of a Saviour. As you read the records of His work, you will find that while He gave His attention, now and then, to condemnation and judgment, most of His arduous days were spent in the work of a Saviour. May I emphasise just this one point? We slip altogether too easily into the attitude of judges. We see people who are bad and we judge them. Meanness

and sin should be rebuked, but people who are lost
in the wild labyrinths of sinful habit need to be
redeemed. We should make much greater progress
if we were to take Jesus' attitude and give ourselves to the business of assisting Him in His beautiful work of redeeming lost souls. People do not
need to be judged half so much as they need to be
loved. People do not need to be criticised adversely
nearly so much as they need to have Christian
sympathy. People, bad people, lost people, will
respond in an amazing percentage of instances to
an appeal for clean Christian living when the appeal
comes from the lips of one who has tasted the
romance of that abundant life of which our
Master spoke.

Here is a modern illustration of Jesus' attitude
toward lost people. A special revival campaign
was being held in one of the great Eastern cities.
A girl who had come into the city, lost her way,
married an infamous character, and had settled
down under the eaves of one of the churches,
became interested. She said to her husband, " Let's
go to that meeting tonight." They had no sooner
arrived when the speaker threw himself into a passionate, eloquent portrayal of the Gospel message.
These two people saw themselves in their hopeless
besmirched condition. They also saw Jesus in His
immaculate whiteness. They heard the speaker say,
" You may be like Jesus if you will look to Him."
They made their decision that night to give them-

selves to Christ and beg His forgiveness for the past.

The next Sunday morning they attended the church near which they lived. The pastor that morning gave an invitation for all who had made Christian decisions to come forward and become members of the church. These two hesitated. They knew that the members of that community knew them as vicious people.

During the week the pastor sent some proper workers to visit in this home. They talked with these people just as they believed Jesus would have, if He had been there. They used their personalities for the wonderful work of carrying the spirit of Jesus into a lost home. They persuaded these two people to seek admission into the church the next Sunday morning.

The pastor again gave the invitation and the two arose and started forward. People all over the church were attempting to see these infamous characters. The woman became very highly wrought up nervously. It looked as though she might even become hysterical. Another woman on the opposite side of the church saw the situation, and as the pastor left the pulpit to come down to the altar, this woman, highly educated, beautifully cultured, arose from her seat and came forward. She took her place by the side of the outcast woman. As the pastor came forward, the outcast woman gasped as though she would collapse in her nervousness. The beautiful woman stepped in front of her, put one hand upon one cheek and the other hand upon the other cheek, turned the face of the woman, kissed one cheek and then the other, and thereby reinstated her in decent society.

This is an unusual illustration, you say? Yes, it is, and God forgive us! For it was just another instance of Jesus operating in the body of a highly educated, beautifully cultured woman. The sooner we realise that for some reason, over nineteen hundred years ago, Jesus took off His body and that the only body that He has to use now, which can be seen by those whom we would win, is ours, the sooner the Kingdom of God will come upon earth. Your hands may become His hands, your face may smile down into sin and sorrow with the sympathy and love of Jesus. Your heart may become the dynamic which will change many sordid situations. This gives our work a dignity and a beauty that are beyond compare.

3. Jesus remains the same in His attitude toward children. I have left this to the last because it is the most important. Do you remember what Jesus' attitude was? He was surrounded by captious questioners one day who were attempting to prove that He was a revolutionary man. He saw a little child. He forgot the curs that were barking at His heels for destruction, saw the beauty in the face of the little child, and I think He must have placed His hand upon the little head, for He was a great

teacher and He would know that when you place your hand upon the head of a child, your fingers touch the hearts of the parents. " Forbid them not to come unto Me," said Jesus, " for of such is the kingdom of heaven."

Let us get the whole suggestion here. Some of us have been under the influence of a heresy, one of the worst heresies that has ever attacked the Christian Church. We have thought that a child had to be converted. Notice what Jesus says. He says: " For of such is the Kingdom of Heaven." What does He mean? Just precisely what He says. Children are Christians, children do not need to be converted unless we allow them to go astray. This is a big challenge to the home and to the church. It is the business of parents and of churches to keep children so near Jesus through Christian nurture and example that they will never become lost.

Bishop Edwin Holt Hughes has told a story which illustrated the value of childhood. A family living somewhere in the Middle West had but one child. He was about at the age of maturity when he came to his father one day and said, " Dad, I would like to go to college. I have felt for some time that if I were trained I might become of some public service."

" John, we are poor," his father replied, " and the crops have been bad for two years. I do not know how we would arrange to meet the expense, but I will go in and talk it over with mother."

He was gone but a few moments when he came out and called John. If you want to discover severe economy, appeal to a mother in the interest of her son. Mother had decided that John could go to college.

After the old gentleman had uttered his homely words of advice, and the crooked fingers of the old mother, made crooked in long and loving service for her son, had gathered together her loving gifts, John went off across country to college. He worked almost night and day for three years and a half, and then wrote back to his parents to come down to college, that he would be graduated but once, that they must come. The old folks wrote to John saying, " We have never been among college people. We haven't the right kind of clothes. We would disgrace you, John. Furthermore, we couldn't get any one to do the chores."

John wrote again and said, " Dad, you must come," and when a boy tells his Dad that he must do something, usually something happens; so the old gentleman hitched up the old gray horse to the carriage and drove down to the college town. John saw them coming, ran down through the streets and threw his arms about the shoulders of his father and mother as though they were a prince and princess. He took them up and down the campus and introduced them to his colleagues and professors as though they were the most eminent people on earth.

John had won the honours of his class. Class Day arrived. They had built a great platform out of doors and arranged seats for the Class Day program. It was John's privilege to deliver the oration. He placed two chairs down in front of the platform for his mother and father, and finally arose a beautiful testimony to a Christian home, a Christian church and a Christian college. Again and again he was interrupted by applause. The old gentleman was finding it difficult to hide his pride. His old hand was gripping the arm of the chair with all the strength that he had left. Just before the conclusion of the oration John was interrupted again, but before he could continue, the old gentleman arose, placed his hand upon his wife's shoulder and said, " Mary, that is the best crop we ever raised." The best crop that any institution can raise upon the face of the earth is a generation of boys and girls who have been kept close to the face, the heart, and the program of Jesus.

This is Jesus' richest field of evangelism, for evangelism has to do not only with the saving of those who are lost, but with the saving of those who are saved; and there never was a time in the history of the world when it was quite so necessary to give attention to this kind of a product. The world needs a generation of boys and girls now who more nearly approximate Jesus' ideal of world citizenship than ever before. America stands in a place of great opportunity to supply this need, but she will fail to meet it unless her boys and girls are kept closer to Christ than any other generation in the history of the human race.

May we emulate Jesus here, and all be evangelists who will place the most emphasis upon the conservation of the fragrant beauties and potential passions of childhood. This is the message of the Changeless Christ to those who would succeed in evangelism.

THE END